Great Recipes
FROM AROUND
the World

Great Recipes
FROM AROUND
the World

SARAH GATES

OVER 130 EASY-TO-COOK
INTERNATIONAL DISHES

SMITHMARK

This edition published in 1994 by
SMITHMARK Publishers Inc.,
a division of US Media Holdings Inc.,
16 East 32nd Street,
New York, NY 10016

SMITHMARK books are available for bulk purchase for sales and
promotion and premium use. For details write or call the manager of
special sales,
SMITHMARK Publishers Inc.
16 East 32nd Street
New York
NY 100016
(212) 532-6616

ISBN 0 8317-5654-3

Editorial Director: Joanna Lorenz
Series Editor: Linda Fraser
Designer: Tony Paine
Photographer: Steve Baxter
Food for Photography: Wendy Lee
Props Stylist: Blake Minton

Printed and bound in Singapore

CONTENTS

SOUPS

Cooking up a selection of soups from around the world was like taking a world cruise without moving an inch from the stove! The kitchen became filled with a glorious succession of the smells of herbs, spices and savory ingredients that go into creating the unique flavors of the popular classics. This selection of hot and cold favorites will give you a taste of the countries they come from. From the sunny Mediterranean comes a hearty Italian Minestrone topped with Pesto Toasts. The flavors of the Far East are captured in a delicious mildly spicy Chicken Soup from Thailand. There's a tasty Rich Tomato Soup from Great Britain for all tomato lovers, and the New England Spiced Pumpkin Soup is the perfect winter warmer.

MINESTRONE WITH PESTO TOASTS

This Italian mixed vegetable soup comes originally from Genoa, but the vegetables vary from region to region. This is also a great way to use up left-over vegetables.

---INGREDIENTS---

Serves 4
2 tbsp olive oil
2 garlic cloves, crushed
1 onion, halved and sliced
2 cups diced lean bacon
2 small zucchini, quartered
  and sliced
½ cup green beans, chopped
2 small carrots, diced
2 celery stalks, finely chopped
bouquet garni
½ cup short cut macaroni
½ cup frozen peas
7oz can red kidney beans, drained
  and rinsed
1 cup shredded green cabbage
4 tomatoes, peeled and seeded
salt and black pepper

For the toasts
8 slices French bread
1 tbsp ready-made pesto sauce
1 tbsp grated Parmesan cheese

1 Heat the oil in a large pan and gently fry the garlic and onion for 5 minutes, until just softened. Add the bacon, zucchini, green beans, carrots and celery to the pan and stir-fry for a further 3 minutes.

2 Pour 5 cups cold water over the vegetables and add the bouquet garni. Cover the pan and simmer for about 25 minutes.

3 Add the macaroni, peas and kidney beans and cook for 8 minutes. Then add the cabbage and tomatoes and cook for a further 5 minutes.

4 Meanwhile, spread the bread slices with the pesto, sprinkle a little Parmesan over each one and brown lightly under a hot broiler.

5 Remove the bouquet garni, season the soup and serve with the toasts.

COOK'S TIP
If you like, to appeal to children, you could replace the macaroni with colored pasta shapes such as shells, twists or bows.

CORN AND SHELLFISH CHOWDER

Chowder comes from the French word *chaudron* meaning a large cooking pot. This is what the fishermen on the east coast of the United States used for boiling up whatever was left over from their catch for supper.

INGREDIENTS

Serves 4
2 tbsp butter
1 small onion, chopped
12oz can corn kernels, drained
2½ cups milk
6oz can white crabmeat, drained and flaked
1 cup cooked, peeled shrimp
2 scallions, finely chopped
⅔ cup light cream
pinch of cayenne pepper
salt and black pepper
4 whole shrimp in shells, to garnish

1 Melt the butter in a large saucepan and gently fry the onion for 4–5 minutes, until softened.

2 Reserve 2 tbsp of the corn for the garnish and add the remainder to the pan with the milk. Bring the soup to a boil, then reduce the heat, cover the pan and simmer over a low heat for 5 minutes.

3 Pour the soup, in several batches if necessary, into a blender or food processor and whizz until smooth.

4 Return the soup to the pan and stir in the crabmeat, shrimp, scallions, cream and cayenne pepper. Reheat gently over a low heat.

5 Meanwhile, place the reserved corn kernels in a small frying pan without oil and dry-fry over a medium heat until golden and toasted.

6 Season the soup well and serve each bowlful topped with a few of the toasted kernels and a whole shrimp.

RICH TOMATO SOUP

An all-time favorite – this fresh soup tastes so much nicer than the canned version. Make sure you use good-flavored, ripe tomatoes, or home-grown.

INGREDIENTS

Serves 4
2lb (about 12 medium) tomatoes
1 tbsp olive oil
1 large onion, chopped
1 garlic clove, crushed
1 potato, chopped
1 tbsp tomato paste
1 tsp sugar
salt and black pepper
4 tbsp sour cream
fresh chervil sprigs, to garnish

1 Place the tomatoes in a large heatproof bowl. Cover them with boiling water and leave to stand for about 1–2 minutes.

2 Heat the olive oil in a large pan and add the onion, garlic and potato. Fry gently for about 5 minutes, until the onion has softened.

3 Meanwhile, drain the hot water from the tomatoes, peel off the skins then halve the tomatoes and remove the cores. Chop the tomato flesh and add to the pan with the seeds, any juice and the tomato paste.

4 Pour over 1¼ cups boiling water, stir, then cover and simmer gently for about 15 minutes, until the potato has softened.

5 Purée the soup in batches in a blender or food processor until smooth. Return the soup to the pan, add the sugar, season well and heat through. Serve in bowls with a dollop of sour cream and the sprigs of fresh chervil.

FRENCH ONION SOUP

INGREDIENTS

Serves 4
2 tbsp butter
1 tbsp oil
3 large onions, thinly sliced
1 tsp soft brown sugar
1 tbsp flour
2 x 10oz cans condensed beef
  consommé
2 tbsp medium sherry
2 tsp Worcestershire sauce
8 slices French bread
1 tbsp French coarse grained mustard
1 cup Gruyère cheese, grated
salt and black pepper
1 tbsp chopped fresh parsley, to garnish

1 Heat the butter and oil in a large pan and add the onions and brown sugar. Cook gently for about 20 minutes, stirring occasionally, until the onions start to turn golden brown.

2 Stir in the flour and cook for a further 2 minutes. Pour in the consommé, plus two cans of water, then add the sherry and Worcestershire sauce. Season well, cover and simmer gently for a further 25–30 minutes.

3 Preheat the broiler and, just before serving, toast the bread lightly on both sides. Spread one side of each slice with the mustard and top with the grated cheese. Grill the toasts until bubbling and golden.

4 Ladle the soup into bowls. Pop two croûtons on top of each bowl of soup and garnish with chopped fresh parsley. Serve at once.

CHILLED LEEK AND POTATO SOUP

This creamy, chilled soup is a version of the *vichyssoise* originally created by a French chef at the Ritz Carlton Hotel in New York to celebrate the opening of the roof gardens.

INGREDIENTS

Serves 4
2 tbsp butter
1 tbsp vegetable oil
1 small onion, chopped
3 leeks, sliced
2 potatoes, diced
2½ cups vegetable stock
1¼ cups milk
3 tbsp light cream
a little extra milk (optional)
salt and black pepper
4 tbsp natural yogurt and a few snipped chives, to garnish

1 Heat the butter and oil in a large pan and add the onion, leeks and potatoes. Cover and simmer for 15 minutes, stirring occasionally. Stir in the stock and milk and simmer for 10 minutes, until the potatoes are tender.

2 Ladle the vegetables and liquid into a blender or food processor in batches and purée until smooth. Return the soup to the pan, stir in the cream and season well.

3 Leave the soup to cool, and then chill for 3–4 hours, or until really cold. You may need to add a little extra milk to thin down the soup, as it will thicken slightly as it cools.

4 Serve the chilled soup in individual bowls, topped with a spoonful of natural yogurt and a sprinkling of snipped fresh chives.

CURRIED PARSNIP SOUP

The spices impart a delicious, mild curry flavor which carries an exotic breath of India.

INGREDIENTS

Serves 4
2 tbsp butter
1 garlic clove, crushed
1 onion, chopped
1 tsp ground cumin
1 tsp ground coriander
3½ cups (about 4) parsnips, sliced
2 tsp medium curry paste
1⅞ cups chicken stock
1⅞ cups milk
4 tbsp sour cream
squeeze of lemon juice
salt and black pepper
fresh coriander sprigs, to garnish
ready-made garlic and coriander naan bread, to serve

1 Heat the butter in a large pan and add the garlic and onion. Fry gently for 4–5 minutes, until lightly golden. Stir in the spices and cook for a further 1–2 minutes.

2 Add the parsnips and stir until well coated with the butter, then stir in the curry paste, followed by the stock. Cover the pan and simmer for 15 minutes, until the parsnips are tender.

3 Ladle the soup into a blender or food processor and whizz until smooth. Return to the pan and stir in the milk. Heat gently for 2–3 minutes, then add 2 tbsp of the sour cream and the lemon juice. Season well.

4 Serve in bowls topped with spoonfuls of the remaining sour cream and the fresh coriander, accompanied by the naan bread.

THAI CHICKEN SOUP

Serves 4

1 tbsp vegetable oil
1 garlic clove, finely chopped
2 x 6oz boned chicken breasts, skinned
   and chopped
½ tsp ground turmeric
¼ tsp hot chili powder
3oz creamed coconut
3¾ cups hot chicken stock
2 tbsp lemon or lime juice
2 tbsp chunky peanut butter
1 cup thread egg noodles,
   broken into small pieces
1 tbsp finely chopped scallions
1 tbsp chopped fresh coriander
salt and black pepper
2 tbsp shredded coconut and
   ½ fresh red chili, seeded and finely
   chopped, to garnish

1 Heat the oil in a large pan and fry the garlic for 1 minute until lightly golden. Add the chicken and spices and stir-fry for a further 3–4 minutes.

2 Crumble the creamed coconut into the hot chicken stock and stir until dissolved. Pour on to the chicken and add the lemon juice, peanut butter and egg noodles.

3 Cover and simmer for about 15 minutes. Add the scallions and fresh coriander, then season well and cook for a further 5 minutes.

4 Meanwhile, place the coconut and chili in a small frying pan and heat for 2–3 minutes, stirring frequently, until the coconut is lightly browned.

5 Serve the soup in bowls sprinkled with the fried coconut and chili.

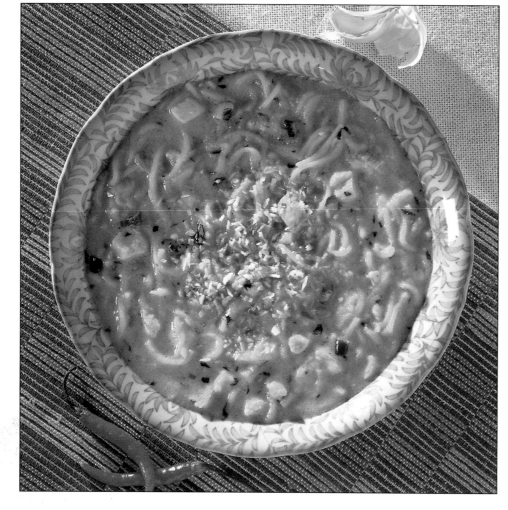

NEW ENGLAND SPICED PUMPKIN SOUP

Serves 4

2 tbsp butter
1 onion, finely chopped
1 small garlic clove, crushed
1 tbsp flour
pinch of grated nutmeg
½ tsp ground cinnamon
3 cups seeded, peeled and cubed
  pumpkin
2½ cups chicken stock
⅔ cup orange juice
1 tsp brown sugar
1 tbsp vegetable oil
2 slices whole grain bread, crusts
  removed
2 tbsp sunflower seeds
salt and black pepper

1 Heat the butter in a large pan, add the onions and garlic and fry gently for 4–5 minutes, until softened.

2 Stir in the flour, spices and pumpkin, then cover and cook gently for 6 minutes, stirring occasionally.

3 Pour in the chicken stock and orange juice and add the brown sugar. Cover and bring to a boil, then reduce the heat and simmer for 20 minutes, until the pumpkin has softened.

4 Pour half of the mixture into a blender or food processor and whizz until smooth. Return the soup to the pan with the remaining chunky mixture, stirring constantly. Season well and heat through.

5 Meanwhile, make the croûtons. Heat the oil in a frying pan, cut the bread into cubes and fry gently until just beginning to brown. Add the sunflower seeds and fry for 1–2 minutes. Drain the croûtons on paper towel.

6 Serve the soup hot with a few of the croûtons scattered over the top. Serve the rest separately.

APPETIZERS AND SNACKS

How often have you set out to prepare a meal and not known what to start with, or felt like eating something deliciously different and run out of inspiration? This section offers you a globetrotter's range of recipes. There are ideal dinner party appetizers, like the delicious Pork and Shrimp Toasts from the Far East, and the French Goat Cheese Salad, as well as filling family snacks like the Tex-Mex Baked Potatoes with Chili, Mediterranean Garlic Toast, or wedges of hot Spanish Omelet. Mexican Dip with Chili Chips makes the perfect speedy snack or appetizer, and when light lunches are called for either Golden Cheese Puffs served with a salad or Kansas City Fritters with tomato salsa are the ideal answer.

INDIAN CURRIED LAMB SAMOSAS

INGREDIENTS

Serves 4

1 tbsp oil
1 garlic clove, crushed
6oz ground lamb
4 scallions, finely chopped
2 tsp medium curry paste
4 ready-to-eat dried apricots,
  chopped
1 small potato, diced
2 tsp apricot chutney
2 tbsp frozen peas
good squeeze of lemon juice
1 tbsp fresh chopped coriander
8oz puff pastry
beaten egg, to glaze
1 tsp cumin seeds
salt and black pepper
3 tbsp natural yogurt and 1 tbsp
  chopped fresh mint, to serve
fresh mint sprigs, to garnish

1 Preheat the oven to 425°F and dampen a large, non-stick baking tray or sheet.

2 Heat the oil in a frying pan and fry the garlic for 30 seconds, then add the ground lamb. Continue frying for about 5 minutes, stirring frequently until the meat is well browned.

3 Stir in the scallions, curry paste, apricots and potato, and cook for 2–3 minutes. Add the apricot chutney, peas and 4 tbsp water. Cover and simmer for 10 minutes, stirring occasionally. Stir in the lemon juice and chopped coriander, season, remove from the heat and leave to cool.

4 On a floured surface, roll out the pastry and cut into four 6in squares. Place a quarter of the curry mixture in the center of each pastry square and brush the edges with beaten egg. Fold over to make a triangle and seal the edges. Knock up the edges with the back of a knife and make a small slit in the top of each.

5 Brush each samosa with beaten egg and sprinkle over the cumin seeds. Place on the damp baking sheet and bake for 20 minutes. Serve with yogurt and mint and garnish with mint sprigs.

MEXICAN DIP WITH CHILI CHIPS

INGREDIENTS

Serves 4

2 medium ripe avocados
juice of 1 lime
½ small onion, finely chopped
½ red chili, seeded and finely chopped
3 tomatoes, peeled, seeded and
  chopped
2 tbsp chopped fresh coriander
2 tbsp sour cream
salt and black pepper
1 tbsp sour cream and a pinch of
  cayenne pepper, to garnish

For the chips
5oz bag tortilla chips
2 tbsp finely grated sharp Cheddar
  cheese
¼ tsp chili powder
2 tbsp chopped fresh parsley

1 Halve and pit the avocados and remove the flesh with a spoon, scraping the shells well.

2 Place the flesh in a blender or food processor with the remaining ingredients and pulse until fairly smooth. Transfer to a bowl, cover and chill.

3 Meanwhile, preheat the broiler, then scatter the tortilla chips over a baking sheet. Mix the grated cheese with the chili powder, sprinkle over the chips and broil for 1–2 minutes, until the cheese has melted.

4 Remove the avocado dip from the fridge, top with the sour cream and sprinkle with cayenne pepper. Serve the bowl on a plate surrounded by the tortilla chips sprinkled with the fresh parsley.

PORK AND SHRIMP TOASTS

A popular appetizer in China and Thailand. Serve the toasts piping hot with a bowl of sweet chili dipping sauce.

INGREDIENTS

Serves 4
4oz ground pork
1 cup cooked, peeled shrimp
1 garlic clove, crushed
2 scallions, finely chopped
2 tbsp chopped fresh coriander
1 egg white, lightly beaten
1 tsp light soy sauce
1 tsp grated lemon rind
4 slices white bread, crusts removed
4 tbsp sesame seeds
oil, for frying
lemon wedges, to serve
fresh coriander sprigs, to garnish

1 Place the pork, shrimp, garlic, scallions, coriander, egg white, soy sauce and lemon rind in a food processor or blender and pulse until the mixture is fairly smooth.

2 Flatten the bread slices with a rolling pin, then spread about one-quarter of the pork and shrimp mixture on each slice, pressing down well. Cut each slice of bread into four triangles.

3 Sprinkle the sesame seeds in a shallow bowl and coat the triangles meat-side down with the seeds.

4 Heat ½in oil in a frying pan until a cube of bread browns in 30 seconds. Fry the toasts meat side down for 3–4 minutes, then turn them over and fry for 2 minutes. Drain on paper towel and serve hot, with lemon wedges, and coriander, to garnish.

MEDITERRANEAN GARLIC TOAST

Mediterranean garlic toast, or *bruschetta*, is served as an appetizer in Spain, Greece and Italy. With a tasty topping of plum tomatoes, mozzarella cheese and salami, it makes a filling snack.

INGREDIENTS

Serves 4
5oz mozzarella cheese, drained
2 plum tomatoes
½ French loaf
1 garlic clove, halved
2 tbsp olive oil, plus extra for brushing
12 small salami slices
1 tbsp fresh torn basil, or
  1 tsp dried basil
salt and black pepper
fresh basil sprigs, to garnish

1 Preheat the broiler to a medium heat. Cut the mozzarella cheese into twelve slices and each tomato into six slices. Cut the French bread in half and slice each half horizontally.

2 Place the bread under the broiler, cut side up, and toast lightly. While the bread is still warm, rub the cut sides of the garlic clove on each cut side of the bread, then drizzle over about ½ tbsp of the olive oil.

3 Top each toast with three slices of tomato, three slices of mozzarella and three slices of salami. Brush the tops with a little more olive oil, season well and sprinkle over the basil.

4 Return to the broiler and toast for 2–3 minutes, until the cheese has melted. Remove and serve hot, garnished with sprigs of fresh basil.

ENGLISH PLOUGHMAN'S PÂTÉ

INGREDIENTS

Serves 4

3 tbsp whole milk farmers' cheese
¾ cup grated mild Cheddar cheese
¾ cup grated Double Gloucester cheese
4 pickled onions, drained and
   finely chopped
1 tbsp apricot chutney
2 tbsp butter, melted
2 tbsp snipped fresh chives
salt and black pepper
4 slices soft cracked wheat bread
watercress and cherry tomatoes,
   to serve

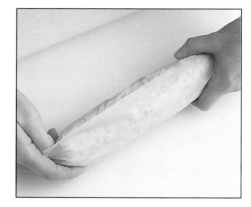

1 Mix together the farmers' cheese, grated cheeses, onions, chutney and butter in a bowl and season lightly.

2 Spoon the mixture on to a sheet of waxed paper and roll up into a cylinder, smoothing the mixture into a roll with your hands. Scrunch the ends of the paper together and twist to seal. Pop in the freezer for about 30 minutes, until just firm.

3 Spread the chives on a plate, then unwrap the chilled cheese pâté. Roll in the chives until evenly coated. Wrap in plastic wrap and chill for 10 minutes.

4 Preheat the broiler. Toast the bread lightly on both sides. Cut off the crusts and slice each piece in half horizontally. Cut each half into two triangles. Broil, untoasted side up, until golden and curled at the edges.

5 Slice the pâté into rounds and serve three or four rounds per person with the Melba toast, watercress and cherry tomatoes.

GOLDEN CHEESE PUFFS

Serve these deep-fried puffs –
called *aigrettes* in France – with
a fruity chutney and salad.

INGREDIENTS

Makes 8
½ cup flour
1 tbsp butter
1 egg, plus 1 egg yolk
1 cup finely grated sharp Cheddar
   cheese
1 tbsp grated Parmesan cheese
½ tsp mustard powder
pinch of cayenne pepper
oil, for frying
salt and black pepper

1 Sift the flour on to a square of
waxed paper and set aside. Place the
butter and ⅔ cup water in a pan and
heat gently until the butter
has melted.

2 Bring the liquid to a boil and tip in
the flour all at once. Remove from
the heat and stir well with a wooden
spoon until the mixture begins to leave
the sides of the pan and forms a ball.
Allow to cool slightly.

3 Beat the egg and egg yolk together
in a bowl with a fork and then
gradually add to the mixture in the
pan, beating well after each addition.

4 Stir the cheeses, mustard powder
and cayenne pepper into the
mixture and season well.

5 Heat the oil in a pan to 375°F or
until a cube of bread browns in 30
seconds. Drop four spoonfuls of the
cheese mixture at a time into the oil
and deep-fry for 2–3 minutes until
golden. Drain on paper towel and keep
hot in the oven while cooking the
remaining mixture. Serve two puffs per
person with a spoonful of mango
chutney and green salad.

FRENCH GOAT CHEESE SALAD

INGREDIENTS

Serves 4
7oz bag prepared mixed salad leaves
4 strips bacon
16 thin slices French bread
4oz goat cheese

For the dressing
4 tbsp olive oil
1 tbsp tarragon vinegar
2 tsp walnut oil
1 tsp Dijon mustard
1 tsp whole grain mustard

1 Preheat the broiler to a medium heat. Rinse and dry the salad leaves, then arrange in four individual bowls. Place the ingredients for the dressing in a screw-topped jar, shake together well and reserve.

2 Lay the bacon strips on a board, then stretch with the back of a knife and cut each into four. Roll each piece up and broil for about 2–3 minutes.

3 Meanwhile, slice the goat cheese into eight and halve each slice. Top each slice of bread with a piece of goat cheese and pop under the broiler. Turn over the bacon and continue cooking with the goat cheese toasts until the cheese is golden and bubbling.

4 Arrange the bacon rolls and toasts on top of the prepared salad leaves, shake the dressing well and pour a little of the dressing over each one.

COOK'S TIP
If you prefer, just slice the goat cheese and place on toasted French bread. Or use whole wheat toast for a delicious nutty flavor.

GREEK SALAD PITAS

Horiatiki is the Greek name for this classic salad made with Feta – a cheese made from sheeps' milk. Try serving the salad in hot pita breads with a minty yogurt dressing.

INGREDIENTS

Makes 4
1 cup diced Feta cheese
¼ cucumber, peeled and diced
8 cherry tomatoes, quartered
½ small green bell pepper, seeded and thinly sliced
¼ small onion, thinly sliced
8 black olives, pitted and halved
2 tbsp olive oil
1 tsp dried oregano
4 large pita breads
4 tbsp natural yogurt
1 tsp dried mint
salt and black pepper
fresh mint, to garnish

1 Place the cheese, cucumber, tomatoes, pepper, onion and olives in a bowl. Stir in the olive oil and oregano, then season well and reserve.

2 Place the pita breads in a toaster or under a preheated broiler for about 2 minutes, until puffed up. Meanwhile, to make the dressing, mix the yogurt with the mint, season well and reserve.

3 Holding the hot pitas in a dish towel, slice each one from top to bottom down one of the longest sides and open out to form a pocket.

4 Divide the prepared salad among the pita breads and drizzle over a spoonful of the dressing. Serve the pittas immediately, garnished with the fresh mint.

KANSAS CITY FRITTERS

Makes 8

1¼ cups canned corn kernels, drained
2 eggs, separated
6 tbsp flour
5 tbsp milk
1 small zucchini, grated
2 strips bacon, diced
2 scallions, finely chopped
good pinch of cayenne pepper
3 tbsp sunflower oil
salt and black pepper
fresh coriander sprigs, to garnish

For the salsa

3 tomatoes, peeled, seeded and diced
½ small red bell pepper, seeded
 and diced
½ small onion, diced
1 tbsp lemon juice
1 tbsp chopped fresh coriander
dash of Tabasco sauce
salt and black pepper

1 To make the salsa, place all the ingredients in a bowl, mix well and season. Cover and chill.

2 Empty the corn into a large bowl and mix in the egg yolks. Add the flour and blend in with a wooden spoon. When the mixture thickens, gradually blend in the milk.

3 Stir in the grated zucchini, bacon, scallions, cayenne pepper and seasoning and set aside.

4 Place the egg whites in a clean bowl and whisk until stiff. Gently fold into the corn batter mixture with a metal spoon.

5 Heat 2 tbsp of the oil in a large frying pan and place four large spoonfuls of the mixture into the oil. Fry on a moderate heat for 2–3 minutes on each side until golden, then drain on paper towel. Keep warm in the oven while frying the remaining four fritters, adding 1 tbsp oil if necessary.

6 Serve two fritters each, garnished with coriander sprigs and a spoonful of the chilled tomato salsa.

TEX-MEX BAKED POTATOES WITH CHILI

Serves 4

2 large potatoes
1 tbsp oil
1 garlic clove, crushed
1 small onion, chopped
½ red bell pepper, seeded and chopped
8oz lean ground beef
½ small fresh red chili, seeded
  and chopped
1 tsp ground cumin
pinch of cayenne pepper
7oz can chopped tomatoes
2 tbsp tomato paste
½ tsp dried oregano
½ tsp dried marjoram
7oz can red kidney beans, drained
1 tbsp chopped fresh coriander
salt and black pepper
4 tbsp sour cream, to serve
chopped fresh parsley, to garnish

1 Preheat the oven to 425°F. Rub the potatoes with a little oil and pierce with skewers. Bake them on the top shelf of the oven for 30 minutes before beginning to cook the chili.

2 Heat the oil in a pan and add the garlic, onion and pepper. Fry gently for 4–5 minutes, until softened.

3 Add the beef and fry until browned all over, then stir in the chili, cumin, cayenne pepper, tomatoes, tomato paste, 4 tbsp water and the herbs. Cover and simmer for about 25 minutes, stirring occasionally.

4 Remove the lid, stir in the kidney beans and cook for 5 minutes. Turn off the heat and stir in the chopped coriander. Season well and set aside.

5 Cut the baked potatoes in half and place them in serving bowls. Top with the chili mixture and a dollop of sour cream and garnish with chopped fresh parsley.

SCRAMBLED EGG AND SALMON MUFFINS

A traditional British breakfast dish – delicious when piled high on top of a hot toasted whole wheat muffin.

INGREDIENTS

Serves 4
4 eggs
3 tbsp light cream or half-and-half
4 whole wheat muffins
2 tbsp butter, plus a little extra for spreading
1 tbsp snipped fresh chives
½ tsp grated lemon rind
4oz smoked salmon or trout, sliced into strips
salt and black pepper
snipped fresh chives, to garnish

1 Break the eggs into a bowl, pour on the cream or half-and-half and season well. Beat lightly with a fork.

2 Halve the muffins and broil until lightly toasted on both sides. Spread with a little butter and keep warm.

3 Meanwhile, melt the butter in a saucepan over a gentle heat, add the eggs and stir occasionally with a wooden spoon until just beginning to set.

4 Add the chives, lemon rind and smoked salmon or trout and stir until just set but still moist. Spoon on to the toasted muffins and garnish with snipped chives. Serve at once.

COOK'S TIP
Don't overcook the scrambled eggs – remove the pan from the heat while they are still quite creamy in texture.

SPANISH OMELET

A traditional Spanish omelet consists of potato, onion and egg and is served as *tapas* or bar food. With mixed peppers and spicy sausage, it makes a filling lunchtime snack.

INGREDIENTS

Serves 4
4 tbsp olive oil
1 small onion, thinly sliced
1 small red bell pepper, seeded and sliced
1 small yellow bell pepper, seeded and sliced
1 large potato, peeled, boiled and diced
1 cup sliced Chorizo sausage
4 eggs
salt and black pepper
chopped fresh parsley, to garnish

1 Heat 2 tbsp of the oil in a frying pan, add the onion and peppers and cook for 7 minutes, stirring occasionally until softened.

2 Add the remaining oil, potato and sausage and cook for a further 3–4 minutes. Reduce the heat slightly.

3 Place the eggs in a bowl, season well and beat lightly with a fork. Pour the eggs over the vegetable and sausage mixture and shake the pan gently.

4 Cook gently for about 5–6 minutes, until beginning to set. Place an upturned plate on top of the pan and carefully turn the omelet upside-down on to the plate.

5 Slide the omelet back into the pan and continue cooking for a further 3 minutes, until the center is just set but still moist. Sprinkle with parsley, cut into wedges and serve straight from the pan.

FRENCH FRIED FISH STICKS

Serves 4
4 tbsp mayonnaise
2 tbsp natural yogurt
grated rind of ½ lemon
squeeze of lemon juice
1 tbsp chopped fresh parsley
1 tbsp chopped capers
2 x 6oz sole fillets, skinned
2 x 6oz plaice fillets, skinned
1 egg, lightly beaten
2 cups fresh white bread crumbs
1 tbsp sesame seeds
pinch of paprika
salt and black pepper
oil, for frying
4 lemon wedges, to serve
watercress, to garnish

1 To make the lemon mayonnaise, mix together the mayonnaise, yogurt, lemon rind and juice, parsley and capers in a bowl. Cover and chill.

2 Cut the fish fillets into thin strips. Place the beaten egg in one shallow bowl. In another bowl, mix together the bread crumbs, sesame seeds, paprika and seasoning.

3 Dip the fish strips, one at a time, into the beaten egg, then into the bread crumb mixture and toss until coated evenly. Lay on a clean plate.

4 Heat about 1in of oil in a frying pan until a cube of bread browns in 30 seconds. Deep-fry the strips in batches for 2–3 minutes, until they are lightly golden in color.

5 Remove with a slotted spoon, drain on paper towel and keep warm in the oven while frying the remainder. Garnish with watercress and serve hot with lemon wedges and the chilled lemon mayonnaise.

> COOK'S TIP
> Use any white fish fillets for the sticks – just be sure to cut them into thin strips. You could try a mixture of haddock and cod as an alternative to the sole and plaice.

GARLIC CHILI SHRIMP

In Spain *gambas al ajillo* are traditionally cooked in small earthenware dishes, but a frying pan is just as good.

Serves 4
4 tbsp olive oil
2–3 garlic cloves, finely chopped
½–1 fresh red chili, seeded and
*   finely chopped*
16 cooked, whole shrimp
15ml/1 tbsp chopped fresh parsley
salt and black pepper
lemon wedges and French bread,
*   to serve*

1 Heat the oil in a large frying pan and add the garlic and chili. Stir-fry for about 1 minute, until the garlic begins to turn brown.

2 Add the shrimp and stir-fry for 3–4 minutes, coating them well with the flavored oil.

3 Add the parsley, remove from the heat and serve four shrimp per person in heated bowls, with the flavored oil spooned over them. Serve with lemon wedges for squeezing and French bread to mop up the juices.

MEAT DISHES

This chapter is full of hearty meat-based, main meal dishes, from special-occasion centerpieces to more informal family fare. They range from Mexican Spiced Roast Leg of Lamb spiked with garlic, herbs and spices for an unusual Sunday roast, to a favorite South African dish – Spiced Lamb Pie, an exotic alternative shepherd's pie with a light golden, creamy coconut and egg custard topping. Nor are all-time favorites forgotten, such as Best-Ever American Burgers, Corn Beef and Egg Hash, a hearty Breton Pork and Bean Casserole, Hungarian Beef Goulash with herby dumplings, and a truly delicious Pork and Sausage Sauerkraut from Alsace.

BRETON PORK AND BEAN CASSEROLE

INGREDIENTS

Serves 4
2 tbsp olive oil
1 onion, chopped
2 garlic cloves, chopped
1lb lean shoulder of pork, cubed
12oz lean lamb (preferably leg), trimmed and cubed
8oz coarse pork and garlic sausage, cut into chunks
14oz can chopped tomatoes
2 tbsp red wine
1 tbsp tomato paste
bouquet garni
14oz can cannellini beans, drained
1 cup whole wheat bread crumbs
salt and black pepper
salad and French bread, to serve

1 Preheat the oven to 325°F. Heat the oil in a large flameproof casserole and fry the chopped onion and garlic until softened. Remove with a slotted spoon and reserve.

2 Add the pork, lamb and sausage to the pan and fry on a high heat until browned on all sides. Return the onion and garlic to the pan.

3 Stir in the chopped tomatoes, wine and tomato paste and add 1¼ cups water. Season well and put in the bouquet garni.

4 Cover and bring to a boil, then transfer the casserole to the pre-heated oven and cook for 1½ hours.

5 Remove the bouquet garni, stir in the beans and sprinkle the bread crumbs over the top. Return to the oven, uncovered, for a further 30 minutes, until the top is golden brown. Serve hot with a green salad and French bread to mop up the juices.

COOK'S TIP
Replace the lamb with duck breast, if you like, but be sure to drain off any fat before sprinkling with the bread crumbs.

BAKED PASTA BOLOGNESE

— INGREDIENTS —

Serves 4

2 tbsp olive oil
1 onion, chopped
1 garlic clove, crushed
1 carrot, diced
2 celery stalks, chopped
2 strips bacon, finely chopped
5 button mushrooms, chopped
1lb lean ground beef
½ cup red wine
1 tbsp tomato paste
7oz can chopped tomatoes
sprig of fresh thyme
2 cups dried penne pasta
1¼ cups milk
2 tbsp butter
2 tbsp flour
1 cup cubed mozzarella cheese
4 tbsp finely grated Parmesan cheese
salt and black pepper
a few small fresh basil sprigs,
    to garnish

1 Heat the oil in a pan and fry the onion, garlic, carrot and celery for 6 minutes, until the onion has softened.

2 Add the bacon and continue frying for 3–4 minutes. Stir in the mushrooms, fry for 2 minutes, then add the beef. Fry on a high heat until well browned all over.

3 Pour in the red wine, the tomato paste dissolved in 3 tbsp water, and the tomatoes, then add the thyme and season well. Bring to a boil, cover the pan and simmer gently for about 30 minutes.

4 Preheat the oven to 400°F. Bring a large pan of water to a boil, add a little of the oil and cook the pasta for about 10 minutes.

5 Meanwhile, place the milk, butter and flour in a saucepan, heat gently and whisk continuously with a balloon whisk until thickened. Stir in the mozzarella cheese and 2 tbsp of the grated Parmesan, and season lightly.

6 Drain the pasta when it is ready and stir into the cheese sauce. Uncover the Bolognese sauce and boil rapidly for 2 minutes to reduce the liquid.

7 Spoon the sauce into an ovenproof dish, top with the pasta mixture and sprinkle the remaining 2 tbsp Parmesan cheese evenly over the top. Bake for 25 minutes until golden. Garnish with basil and serve hot.

BEST-EVER AMERICAN BURGERS

─── INGREDIENTS ───

Makes 4 burgers

1 tbsp vegetable oil
1 small onion, finely chopped
1lb ground beef
1 large garlic clove, crushed
1 tsp ground cumin
2 tsp ground coriander
2 tbsp tomato paste or catsup
1 tsp whole grain mustard
dash of Worcestershire sauce
2 tbsp chopped fresh mixed herbs
    (parsley, thyme and oregano)
1 tbsp lightly beaten egg
salt and black pepper
flour, for shaping
oil, for frying (optional)
mixed salad, potato chips and
    relish, to serve

1 Heat the oil in a frying pan, add the onion and cook for 5 minutes, until softened. Remove from the pan, drain on paper towel and leave to cool.

2 Mix together the ground beef, garlic, spices, tomato paste or catsup, mustard, Worcestershire sauce, herbs, beaten egg and seasoning in a bowl. Stir in the cooled onion.

3 Sprinkle a board with flour and shape the mixture into four burgers using floured hands and a spatula. Cover and chill for 15 minutes.

4 Heat a little oil in a pan and fry the burgers on a medium heat for about 5 minutes each side, depending on how rare you like them. Alternatively, cook under a medium broiler. Serve with salad, potato chips and relish.

PORK AND SAUSAGE SAUERKRAUT

Juniper and coriander flavor this traditional dish from Alsace.

─── INGREDIENTS ───

Serves 4

2 tbsp vegetable oil
1 large onion, thinly sliced
1 garlic clove, crushed
1lb jar sauerkraut, rinsed well and
    drained
1 eating apple, cored and chopped
5 juniper berries
5 coriander seeds, crushed
1lb piece of lightly smoked pork butt
8oz whole smoked pork sausage,
    pricked
¾ cup unsweetened apple juice
⅔ cup chicken stock
1 bay leaf
8 small potatoes

1 Preheat the oven to 350°F. Heat the oil in a large flameproof casserole and fry the onion and garlic for 3–4 minutes, until softened. Stir in the sauerkraut, apple, juniper berries and coriander seeds.

2 Lay the piece of pork butt and the sausage on top of the sauerkraut, pour on the apple juice and stock and add the bay leaf. Cover and bake in the oven for about 1 hour.

3 Remove from the oven and put the potatoes into the casserole. Add a little more stock if necessary, cover and bake for a further 30 minutes, or until the potatoes are tender.

4 Just before serving, lift out the pork and sausage on to a board and slice. Spoon the sauerkraut on to a warmed platter, top with the meat and surround with the potatoes.

Corn Beef and Egg Hash

This classic American hash is made with corn beef and is a popular brunch or lunchtime dish all over the United States. Serve with chili sauce for a really authentic touch.

INGREDIENTS

Serves 4

2 tbsp vegetable oil
2 tbsp butter
1 onion, finely chopped
1 green bell pepper, seeded and diced
2 large boiled potatoes, diced
12oz can corn beef, cubed
¼ tsp grated nutmeg
¼ tsp paprika
4 eggs
salt and black pepper
chopped fresh parsley, to garnish
sweet chili sauce or tomato sauce,
   to serve

1 Heat the oil and butter together in a large frying pan and add the onion. Fry for 5–6 minutes, until softened.

2 In a bowl, mix together the pepper, potatoes, corn beef, nutmeg and paprika and season well. Add to the pan and toss gently to distribute the cooked onion. Press down lightly and fry on a medium heat for about 3–4 minutes, until a golden brown crust has formed on the bottom.

3 Stir the mixture through to distribute the crust, then repeat the frying twice, until the mixture is well browned.

4 Make four wells in the hash and crack an egg into each one. Cover and cook gently for about 4–5 minutes, until the egg whites are just set.

5 Sprinkle with chopped parsley and cut the hash into quarters. Serve hot with sweet chili sauce.

COOK'S TIP
Put the can of corn beef into the fridge to chill for about half an hour before using – it will firm up and cut into cubes more easily.

HUNGARIAN BEEF GOULASH

Serves 4
2 tbsp vegetable oil
2lb chuck steak, cubed
2 onions, chopped
1 garlic clove, crushed
1 tbsp flour
2 tsp paprika
1 tsp caraway seeds
14oz can chopped tomatoes
1¼ cups beef stock
1 large carrot, chopped
1 red bell pepper, seeded and chopped
sour cream, to serve
pinch of paprika, to garnish

For the dumplings
1 cup self-rising flour
½ cup shredded suet
1 tbsp chopped fresh parsley
½ tsp caraway seeds
salt and black pepper

1 Heat the oil in a flameproof casserole, add the meat and fry over a high heat for 5 minutes, stirring, until browned. Remove with a slotted spoon.

2 Add the onions and garlic and fry gently for 5 minutes, until softened. Add the flour, paprika and caraway seeds, stir and cook for 2 minutes.

3 Return the browned meat to the casserole and stir in the tomatoes and stock. Bring to a boil, cover and simmer gently for 2 hours.

4 Meanwhile, make the dumplings. Sift the flour and seasoning into a bowl, add the suet, parsley, caraway seeds and about 3–4 tbsp water and mix to a soft dough. Divide into eight pieces and roll into balls. Cover and reserve.

5 After 2 hours, stir the carrot and pepper into the goulash and season well. Drop the dumplings into the goulash, cover and simmer for about 25 minutes. Serve in bowls topped with a spoonful of sour cream sprinkled with a pinch of paprika.

PEKING BEEF AND PEPPER STIR-FRY

INGREDIENTS

Serves 4

12oz rump or sirloin steak, sliced
  into strips
2 tbsp soy sauce
2 tbsp medium sherry
1 tbsp cornstarch
1 tsp brown sugar
1 tbsp sunflower oil
1 tbsp sesame oil
1 garlic clove, finely chopped
1 tbsp grated fresh ginger root
1 red bell pepper, seeded and sliced
1 yellow bell pepper, seeded and sliced
4oz sugar snap peas
4 scallions, diagonally cut into
  2in pieces
2 tbsp Chinese oyster sauce
hot noodles, to serve

1 In a bowl, mix together the steak strips, soy sauce, sherry, cornstarch and brown sugar. Cover and leave to marinate for 30 minutes.

2 Heat the oils in a wok or large frying pan. Add the garlic and ginger and stir-fry quickly for about 30 seconds. Add the peppers, sugar snap peas and scallions and stir-fry over a high heat for 3 minutes.

3 Add the beef with the marinade juices to the wok or frying pan and stir-fry for a further 3–4 minutes.

4 Finally, pour in the oyster sauce and 4 tbsp water and stir until the sauce has thickened slightly. Serve immediately with hot noodles.

TEXAN BARBECUED RIBS

An American favorite of pork spare ribs cooked in a sweet and sour barbecue sauce. Ideal as a barbecue dish, this can be just as easily cooked in the oven.

INGREDIENTS

Serves 4

3lb (about 16) lean pork spare ribs
1 onion, finely chopped
1 large garlic clove, crushed
½ cup tomato catsup
2 tbsp orange juice
2 tbsp red wine vinegar
1 tsp mustard
2 tsp honey
2 tbsp soft light brown sugar
dash of Worcestershire sauce
2 tbsp vegetable oil
salt and black pepper
chopped fresh parsley, to garnish

1 Preheat the oven to 400°F. Place the lean pork spare ribs in a large shallow roasting pan and then bake, uncovered, for 20 minutes.

2 Meanwhile, mix together the onion, garlic, tomato catsup, orange juice, red wine vinegar, mustard, honey, brown sugar, Worcestershire sauce, oil and seasoning in a pan. Bring to a boil, then reduce the heat and simmer gently for about 5 minutes.

3 Remove the ribs from the oven and reduce the temperature to 350°F. Spoon over half the sauce, covering the ribs well, and bake for 20 minutes. Turn the ribs over, baste with the remaining sauce and cook in the oven for a further 25 minutes.

4 Sprinkle the ribs with parsley and serve three or four ribs per person. Provide small finger bowls for washing sticky fingers.

TURKISH LAMB AND APRICOT STEW

INGREDIENTS

Serves 4

1 large eggplant, cubed
2 tbsp sunflower oil
1 onion, chopped
1 garlic clove, crushed
1 tsp ground cinnamon
3 whole cloves
1lb boned leg of lamb, cubed
14oz can chopped tomatoes
⅔ cup ready-to-eat dried apricots
4oz canned chick-peas, drained
1 tsp honey
salt and black pepper
3 cups cooked couscous, to serve
2 tbsp olive oil
2 tbsp chopped almonds, fried in a
*   little oil*
chopped fresh parsley

1 Place the eggplant in a colander, sprinkle with salt and leave for 30 minutes. Heat the oil in a flameproof casserole, add the onion and garlic and fry for 5 minutes, until softened.

2 Stir in the ground cinnamon and cloves and fry for 1 minute. Add the lamb and cook for 5–6 minutes, stirring occasionally, until well browned.

3 Rinse, drain and pat dry the eggplant, add to the pan and cook for 3 minutes, stirring well. Add the tomatoes, 1¼ cups water, the apricots and salt and pepper. Bring to a boil, then cover the pan and simmer gently for about 45 minutes.

4 Stir in the chick-peas and honey and cook for a further 15–20 minutes, or until the lamb is tender. Serve the stew accompanied by couscous with the olive oil, fried almonds and chopped parsley stirred in.

THAI PORK SATAY WITH PEANUT SAUCE

Makes 8
½ small onion, finely chopped
2 garlic cloves, crushed
2 tbsp lemon juice
1 tbsp soy sauce
1 tsp ground coriander
½ tsp ground cumin
1 tsp ground turmeric
2 tbsp vegetable oil
1lb pork tenderloin
fresh coriander sprigs, to garnish
boiled rice, to serve

For the sauce
2oz creamed coconut, chopped
4 tbsp chunky peanut butter
1 tbsp lemon juice
½ tsp ground cumin
½ tsp ground coriander
1 tsp soft brown sugar
1 tbsp soy sauce
1–2 dried red chilies, or ½ fresh red
 chili, seeded and finely chopped
1 tbsp chopped fresh coriander (leaves
 and stems)

For the salad
½ small cucumber, peeled and diced
1 tbsp white wine vinegar
1 tbsp chopped fresh coriander
salt and black pepper

1 Soak eight wooden skewers in water for about 30 minutes – this will prevent them charring during broiling.

2 Place the onion, garlic, lemon juice, soy sauce, ground spices and oil into a food processor or blender and pulse until smooth, or mix in a bowl.

3 Cut the pork into thin strips and place in a bowl, spoon over the marinade and mix well. Cover and chill for at least 2 hours.

4 Preheat the broiler to the hottest setting. Thread about two or three pieces of pork on to each skewer and broil on a rack for 2–3 minutes each side, basting once with the marinade.

5 Meanwhile, make the sauce. Dissolve the creamed coconut in ⅔ cup boiling water. Put the remaining ingredients into a pan and stir in the coconut liquid. Bring to a boil, stirring well, and simmer gently for 5 minutes, until thick.

6 Mix together the salad ingredients. Arrange the satay sticks on a platter and garnish with coriander sprigs. Serve with bowls of sauce, salad and rice.

MIDDLE EASTERN LAMB KEBABS

Skewered, broiled meats are the main item in many Middle Eastern and Greek restaurants. In this recipe marinated lamb is broiled with vegetables.

──────── INGREDIENTS ────────

Makes 4
1lb boneless leg of lamb, cubed
5 tbsp olive oil
1 tbsp chopped fresh oregano or thyme,
    or 2 tsp dried oregano
1 tbsp chopped fresh parsley
juice of ½ lemon
½ small eggplant, quartered and
    thickly sliced
4 baby onions, halved
2 tomatoes, quartered
4 fresh bay leaves
salt and black pepper
pita bread and natural yogurt,
    to serve

1 Place the lamb in a bowl. Mix together the olive oil, oregano, parsley, lemon juice and seasoning, pour over the lamb and mix well. Cover and marinate for about 1 hour.

2 Preheat the broiler. Thread the marinated lamb, eggplant, onions, tomatoes and bay leaves alternately on to four large skewers.

3 Place the kebabs on a broiling rack and brush the vegetables liberally with the leftover marinade. Cook the kebabs under a medium heat for about 8–10 minutes on each side, basting once or twice with the juices that have collected in the bottom of the broiling pan. Serve the kebabs hot, with hot pita bread and natural yogurt.

COOK'S TIP
Make a lemony bulgur wheat salad to accompany the kebabs if you like. Or serve them with plain, boiled rice – either basmati or jasmine rice would be a good choice.

MEXICAN SPICED ROAST LEG OF LAMB

──────── INGREDIENTS ────────

Serves 4
1 small leg or half leg (about
    2½ lb) lamb
1 tbsp dried oregano
1 tsp ground cumin
1 tsp hot chili powder
2 garlic cloves
3 tbsp olive oil
2 tbsp red wine vinegar
salt and black pepper
fresh oregano sprigs, to garnish

1 Preheat the oven to 425°F. Place the leg of lamb on a large cutting board.

2 Place the oregano, cumin, chili powder and one of the garlic cloves, crushed, into a bowl. Pour on half of the olive oil and mix well to form a paste. Set the paste aside.

3 Using a sharp knife, make a crisscross pattern of fairly deep slits through the skin and just into the meat.

4 Press the spice paste into the meat slits with the back of a knife.

5 Slice the remaining garlic clove thinly and cut each slice in half again. Push the pieces of garlic deeply into the slits in the meat (to prevent burning during roasting).

6 Mix the vinegar and remaining oil, pour over the joint and season with salt and freshly ground black pepper.

7 Bake the lamb for about 15 minutes at the higher temperature, then reduce the heat to 350°F and cook for a further 1¼ hours (or a little longer if you like your meat well done). Serve the lamb with a delicious gravy made with the spicy pan juices and garnish with fresh oregano sprigs.

BOEUF BOURGUIGNON

This French classic is named after the region it comes from, Burgundy, where the local red wine is used to flavor this delicious stew.

INGREDIENTS

Serves 4

2 tbsp olive oil
8oz piece of slab bacon, cubed
12 whole baby onions
2lb braising steak, cut into 2in squares
1 large onion, sliced
1 tbsp flour
¾ pint red Burgundy wine
bouquet garni
1 garlic clove
8oz button mushrooms, halved
salt and black pepper
chopped fresh parsley, to garnish

1 Heat the oil in a flameproof casserole and add the bacon and onions. Fry for about 7–8 minutes, until the onions have browned and the bacon fat is transparent. Remove with a slotted spoon and reserve.

2 Add the beef to the pan and fry quickly on all sides until browned. Add the sliced onion and continue cooking for 4–5 minutes.

3 Sprinkle over the flour and stir well. Pour over the wine, add the bouquet garni and garlic. Cover and simmer gently for about 2 hours. Stir in the reserved sautéed onions and bacon and add a little extra wine, if necessary.

4 Add the mushrooms. Cover and cook for a further 30 minutes. Remove the bouquet garni and garlic and garnish with chopped fresh parsley.

SPICED LAMB PIE

A quite delicious South African shepherd's pie. The recipe was originally poached from the Afrikaners' Malay slaves, hence the slightly oriental flavor.

INGREDIENTS

Serves 4

1 tbsp vegetable oil
1 medium onion, chopped
1½ lb ground lamb
2 tbsp medium curry paste
2 tbsp mango chutney
2 tbsp lemon juice
4 tbsp chopped, blanched almonds
2 tbsp sultanas
3oz creamed coconut, crumbled
2 eggs
2 bay leaves
salt and black pepper

1 Preheat the oven to 350°F. Heat the oil in a frying pan.

2 Add the onion to the pan and cook for about 5–6 minutes, stirring occasionally, until softened.

3 Add the lamb and cook on a medium heat, turning frequently until browned all over. Stir in the curry paste, chutney, lemon juice, almonds and sultanas, season well and cook for about 5 minutes.

4 Transfer the mixture to an oven-proof dish and cook in the oven, uncovered, for 10 minutes.

5 Meanwhile, dissolve the creamed coconut in ⅞ cup boiling water and cool slightly. Beat in the eggs and a little seasoning.

6 Remove the dish from the oven and pour the coconut custard over the meat mixture. Lay the bay leaves on the top and return the dish to the oven for 30–35 minutes, or until the top is set and golden. Serve hot.

POULTRY AND GAME

Chicken, turkey and game are favorite ingredients in most households and this chapter combines popular classics such as a rich and warming Coq au Vin from Burgundy, and the simple but delicious Normandy Roast Chicken, with some more exotic delights that you will want to cook over and over again. From the heart of Louisiana comes the ultimate chicken 'n' rice dish, Chicken Jambalaya, a great family meal-in-one, and from India comes a Chicken Biryani that will outshine any take-out version. The Country Cider Hot-Pot, studded with succulent prunes, is a great British winter warmer, and the simple pan-fried Crumbed Turkey Steaks, with their crunchy coating and a squeeze of lemon juice, will appeal to all members of the family.

FRENCH-STYLE POT-ROAST POUSSIN

Serves 4

1 tbsp olive oil
1 onion, sliced
1 large garlic clove, sliced
½ cup diced lightly smoked bacon
2 fresh poussin (just under 1lb each)
2 tbsp butter, melted
2 baby celery hearts, each cut into 4
8 baby carrots
2 small zucchini, cut into chunks
8 small new potatoes
2½ cups chicken stock
⅔ cup dry white wine
1 bay leaf
2 fresh thyme sprigs
2 fresh rosemary sprigs
1 tbsp butter, softened
1 tbsp flour
salt and black pepper
fresh herbs, to garnish

1 Preheat the oven to 375°F. Heat the olive oil in a large flameproof casserole and add the onion, garlic and bacon. Sauté for 5–6 minutes, until the onion has softened.

2 Brush the poussin with a little of the melted butter and season well. Lay on top of the onion mixture and arrange the prepared vegetables around them. Pour the chicken stock and wine around the birds and add the herbs.

3 Cover, bake for 20 minutes, then remove the lid and brush the birds with the remaining butter. Bake for a further 25–30 minutes until golden.

4 Transfer the poussin to a warmed serving platter and cut each in half with poultry shears or scissors. Remove the vegetables with a slotted spoon and arrange them round the birds. Cover with foil and keep warm.

5 Discard the herbs from the pan juices. In a bowl mix together the butter and flour to form a paste. Bring the liquid in the pan to a boil and then whisk in teaspoonfuls of the paste until thickened. Season the sauce and serve with the poussin and vegetables, garnished with fresh herbs.

COQ AU VIN

Serves 4

3 tbsp flour
3lb chicken, cut into 8 pieces
1 tbsp olive oil
4 tbsp butter
20 baby onions
3oz piece of slab bacon without rind,
* diced*
about 20 button mushrooms
2 tbsp brandy
1 bottle red Burgundy wine
bouquet garni
3 garlic cloves
1 tsp soft light brown sugar
1 tbsp butter, softened
1 tbsp flour
salt and black pepper
1 tbsp chopped fresh parsley and
* croûtons, to garnish*

1 Place the flour and seasoning in a large plastic bag and shake each chicken piece in it until lightly coated. Heat the oil and butter in a large flame-proof casserole. Add the onions and bacon and sauté for 3–4 minutes, until the onions have browned lightly. Add the mushrooms and fry for 2 minutes. Remove with a slotted spoon, place in a bowl and reserve.

2 Add the chicken pieces to the hot oil and cook until browned on all sides, about 5–6 minutes. Pour in the brandy and (standing well back from the pan) carefully light it with a match, then shake the pan gently until the flames subside. Pour on the wine, add the bouquet garni, garlic, sugar and seasoning.

3 Bring to a boil, cover and simmer for 1 hour, stirring occasionally. Return the reserved onions, bacon and mushrooms to the casserole, cover and cook for a further 30 minutes.

4 Lift out the chicken, vegetables and bacon with a slotted spoon and arrange on a warmed dish.

5 Remove the bouquet garni and boil the liquid rapidly for 2 minutes to reduce slightly. Cream the butter and flour together and whisk in teaspoonfuls of the mixture until the liquid has thickened slightly. Pour this sauce over the chicken and serve garnished with parsley and croûtons.

TANDOORI CHICKEN KEBABS

This dish originates from the plains of the Punjab at the foot of the Himalayas. There food is traditionally cooked in clay ovens known as *tandoors* – hence the name.

── INGREDIENTS ──

Serves 4
4 boneless, skinless chicken breasts
  (about 6oz each)
1 tbsp lemon juice
3 tbsp tandoori paste
3 tbsp natural yogurt
1 garlic clove, crushed
2 tbsp chopped fresh coriander
1 small onion, cut into wedges and
  separated into layers
a little oil, for brushing
salt and black pepper
fresh coriander sprigs, to garnish
rice and naan bread, to serve

1 Chop the chicken breasts into 1in cubes, place in a bowl and add the lemon juice, tandoori paste, yogurt, garlic, coriander and seasoning. Cover and leave to marinate in the fridge for about 2–3 hours.

2 Preheat the broiler. Thread alternate pieces of marinated chicken and onion on to four skewers.

3 Brush the onions with a little oil, lay on a broiling rack and cook under a high heat for 10–12 minutes, turning once. Garnish the kebabs with fresh coriander and serve at once with rice and naan bread.

> COOK'S TIP
> Use boned and skinless chicken thighs, or turkey breasts, for a cheaper alternative.

CHINESE CHICKEN WITH CASHEW NUTS

── INGREDIENTS ──

Serves 4
4 boneless, skinless chicken breasts
  (about 6oz each), sliced into
  thin strips
3 garlic cloves, crushed
4 tbsp soy sauce
2 tbsp cornstarch
8oz dried egg noodles
3 tbsp groundnut or sunflower oil
1 tbsp sesame oil
1 cup roasted cashew nuts
6 scallions, cut into 2in pieces and
  halved lengthwise
scallion curls and a little chopped red
  chili, to garnish

1 Place the chicken in a bowl with the garlic, soy sauce and cornstarch and mix until the chicken is well coated. Cover and chill for about 30 minutes.

2 Meanwhile, bring a pan of water to the boil and add the egg noodles. Turn off the heat and leave to stand for 5 minutes. Drain well and reserve.

3 Heat the oils in a large frying pan or wok and add the chilled chicken and marinade juices. Stir-fry on a high heat for about 3–4 minutes, or until golden brown.

4 Add the cashew nuts and scallions to the pan or wok and stir-fry for 2–3 minutes.

5 Add the drained noodles and stir-fry for a further 2 minutes. Toss the noodles well and serve immediately, garnished with the scallion curls and chopped chili.

CHINESE-STYLE CHICKEN SALAD

INGREDIENTS

Serves 4

4 boneless chicken breasts (about
  6oz each)
4 tbsp dark soy sauce
pinch of Chinese five spice powder
good squeeze of lemon juice
½ cucumber, peeled and cut into
  matchsticks
1 tsp salt
3 tbsp sunflower oil
2 tbsp sesame oil
1 tbsp sesame seeds
2 tbsp dry sherry
2 carrots, cut into matchsticks
8 scallions, shredded
1 cup beansprouts

For the sauce

4 tbsp chunky peanut butter
2 tsp lemon juice
2 tsp sesame oil
¼ tsp hot chili powder
1 scallion, finely chopped

1 Put the chicken portions into a large pan and just cover with water. Add 1 tbsp of the soy sauce, the Chinese five spice powder and lemon juice, cover and bring to a boil, then simmer for about 20 minutes.

2 Meanwhile, place the cucumber matchsticks in a colander, sprinkle with the salt and cover with a plate with a weight on top. Leave to drain for 30 minutes – set the colander in a bowl or on a deep plate to catch the drips.

3 Lift out the poached chicken with a slotted spoon and leave until cool enough to handle. Remove and discard the skins and pound the chicken lightly with a rolling pin to loosen the fibers. Slice into thin strips and reserve.

4 Heat the oils in a large frying pan or wok. Add the sesame seeds, fry for 30 seconds and then stir in the remaining 3 tbsp soy sauce and the sherry. Add the carrots and stir-fry for 2–3 minutes, until just tender. Remove from the heat and reserve.

5 Rinse the cucumber well, pat dry with paper towel and place in a bowl. Add the scallions, beansprouts, cooked carrots, pan juices and shredded chicken, and mix together. Transfer to a shallow dish. Cover and chill for about 1 hour, turning the mixture in the juices once or twice.

6 To make the sauce, cream the peanut butter with the lemon juice, sesame oil and chili powder, adding a little hot water to form a paste, then stir in the scallion. Arrange the chicken mixture on a serving dish and serve with the peanut sauce.

CHICKEN BIRYANI

INGREDIENTS

Serves 4

1½ cups basmati rice, rinsed
½ tsp salt
5 whole cardamom pods
2–3 whole cloves
1 cinnamon stick
3 tbsp vegetable oil
3 onions, sliced
1½lb boneless, skinless chicken
    (4 x 6oz chicken breasts), cubed
¼ tsp ground cloves
5 cardamom pods, seeds removed
    and ground
¼ tsp hot chili powder
1 tsp ground cumin
1 tsp ground coriander
½ tsp freshly ground black pepper
3 garlic cloves, finely chopped
1 tsp finely chopped fresh ginger root
juice of 1 lemon
4 tomatoes, sliced
2 tbsp chopped fresh coriander
⅔ cup natural yogurt
½ tsp saffron strands soaked in 2 tsp
    hot milk
3 tbsp toasted flaked almonds and fresh
    coriander sprigs, to garnish
natural yogurt, to serve

1 Preheat the oven to 375°F. Bring a pan of water to a boil and add the rice, salt, ground cardamom, cloves and cinnamon stick. Boil for 2 minutes and then drain, leaving the whole spices in the rice.

2 Heat the oil in a pan and fry the onions for about 8 minutes, until browned. Add the chicken followed by all the ground spices, the garlic, ginger and lemon juice. Stir-fry for 5 minutes.

3 Transfer the chicken mixture to an ovenproof casserole and lay the tomatoes on top. Sprinkle over the fresh coriander, spoon over the yogurt and top with the drained rice.

4 Drizzle the saffron and milk mixture over the rice and then pour over ⅔ cup water.

5 Cover tightly and bake in the oven for 1 hour. Transfer to a warmed serving platter and remove the whole spices from the rice. Garnish with toasted almonds and fresh coriander and serve with yogurt.

ITALIAN CHICKEN

Serves 4

2 tbsp flour
4 chicken pieces (legs, breasts
  or quarters)
2 tbsp olive oil
1 onion, chopped
2 garlic cloves, chopped
1 red bell pepper, seeded and chopped
14oz can chopped tomatoes,
2 tbsp ready-made pesto sauce
4 sun-dried tomatoes in oil, chopped
⅔ cup chicken stock
1 tsp dried oregano
8 black olives, pitted
salt and black pepper
chopped fresh basil and basil leaves,
  to garnish
tagliatelle, to serve

1 Place the flour and seasoning in a paper bag. Add the chicken pieces and shake well until coated. Heat the oil in a flameproof casserole, add the chicken and brown quickly. Remove the chicken and set aside.

2 Lower the heat, add the onion, garlic and pepper and cook for 5 minutes. Stir in the other ingredients, except the olives, and bring to a boil.

3 Return the sautéed chicken pieces to the casserole, season lightly, cover and simmer for 30–35 minutes, or until the chicken is cooked.

4 Add the olives and simmer for a further 5 minutes. Transfer to a warmed serving dish, sprinkle with the chopped basil and garnish with basil leaves. Serve with hot tagliatelle.

HONEY AND ORANGE GLAZED CHICKEN

This way of cooking chicken breasts is popular in America, Australia and Great Britain. It is ideal for an easy evening meal served with baked potatoes.

Serves 4

4 x 6oz boneless chicken breasts
1 tbsp oil
4 scallions, chopped
1 garlic clove, crushed
3 tbsp honey
4 tbsp fresh orange juice
1 orange, peeled and segmented
2 tbsp soy sauce
fresh lemon balm or flat leaf parsley,
  to garnish
baked potatoes and mixed salad,
  to serve

1 Preheat the oven to 375°F. Place the chicken breasts in a shallow roasting pan and set aside.

2 Heat the oil in a small pan, and fry the scallions and garlic for 2 minutes until softened. Add the honey, orange juice, orange segments and soy sauce to the pan, stirring well until the honey has dissolved.

3 Pour over the chicken and bake, uncovered, for about 45 minutes, basting once or twice until the chicken is cooked. Garnish with lemon balm or parsley and serve the chicken and its sauce with baked potatoes and a salad.

COOK'S TIP
Look out for mustard flavored with honey to add to this dish instead of the honey.

HAMPSHIRE FARMHOUSE TART

INGREDIENTS

Serves 4

2 cups whole wheat flour
4 tbsp butter, cubed
4 tbsp lard
1 tsp caraway seeds
1 tbsp oil
1 onion, chopped
1 garlic clove, crushed
2 cups chopped cooked chicken
2½ cups washed and chopped
   watercress leaves
grated rind of ½ small lemon
2 eggs, lightly beaten
¾ cup heavy cream
3 tbsp natural yogurt
good pinch of grated nutmeg
3 tbsp grated Cheddar cheese
beaten egg, to glaze
salt and black pepper

1 Place the flour in a bowl with a pinch of salt. Add the butter and lard and rub into the flour with your fingertips until the mixture resembles bread crumbs. (Alternatively, you can use a food processor.)

2 Stir in the caraway seeds and 3 tbsp iced water and mix thoroughly to make a firm dough. Knead lightly on a floured surface until smooth.

3 Roll out the pastry on a lightly floured surface and use to line a 7 x 11in loose-based pie pan. Reserve the pastry trimmings. Prick the base and chill for 20 minutes. Place a baking sheet in the oven and preheat to 400°F.

4 Heat the oil in a frying pan and sauté the onion and garlic for 5–6 minutes, until just softened. Remove from the heat and cool.

5 Line the pastry shell with waxed paper and fill with baking beans. Bake for 10 minutes, then remove the paper and beans and cook for a further 5 minutes.

6 Mix together the onion, chicken, watercress and lemon rind and spoon into the tart shell. Beat the eggs, cream, yogurt, nutmeg, cheese and sea-soning and pour over the chicken mix.

7 Roll out the pastry trimmings and cut out ½in strips. Brush with egg, then twist each strip and lay in a lattice over the tart. Press the ends on to the pastry edge. Bake for 35 minutes, until the top is golden. Serve warm or cold.

CAJUN CHICKEN JAMBALAYA

INGREDIENTS

Serves 4

2½lb fresh chicken
1½ onions
1 bay leaf
4 black peppercorns
1 parsley sprig
2 tbsp vegetable oil
2 garlic cloves, chopped
1 green bell pepper, seeded and
    chopped
1 celery stalk, chopped
1¼ cups long grain rice
1 cup Chorizo sausage, sliced
1 cup chopped cooked ham
14oz can chopped tomatoes with herbs
½ tsp hot chili powder
½ tsp cumin seeds
½ tsp ground cumin
1 tsp dried thyme
1 cup cooked, peeled shrimp
dash of Tabasco sauce
chopped parsley, to garnish

1 Place the chicken in a large flame-proof casserole and pour over 2½ cups water. Add the half onion, the bay leaf, peppercorns and parsley and bring to a boil. Cover and simmer gently for about 1½ hours.

2 When the chicken is cooked lift it out of the stock, remove the skin and carcass and chop the meat. Strain the stock, leave to cool and reserve.

3 Chop the remaining onion and heat the oil in a large frying pan. Add the onion, garlic, green pepper and celery. Fry for about 5 minutes, then stir in the rice coating the grains with the oil. Add the sausage, ham and reserved chopped chicken and fry for a further 2–3 minutes, stirring frequently.

4 Pour in the tomatoes and 1¼ cups of the reserved stock and add the chili, cumin and thyme. Bring to a boil, then cover and simmer gently for 20 minutes, or until the rice is tender and the liquid absorbed.

5 Stir in the shrimp and Tabasco. Cook for a further 5 minutes, then season well and serve hot, garnished with chopped parsley.

NORMANDY ROAST CHICKEN

Serves 4
4 tbsp butter, softened
2 tbsp chopped fresh tarragon
1 small garlic clove, crushed
3lb fresh chicken
1 tsp flour
⅔ cup light cream or crème fraîche
good squeeze of lemon juice
salt and black pepper
fresh tarragon and lemon slices,
*   to garnish*

1 Preheat the oven to 400°F. Mix together the butter, 1 tbsp of the chopped tarragon, the garlic and seasoning in a bowl. Spoon half the butter into the cavity of the chicken.

2 Carefully lift the skin at the neck end of the bird away from the breast flesh on each side, then gently push a little of the butter into each pocket and smooth down over the breast with your fingers.

3 Season the bird and lay it, breast down, in a roasting pan. Roast in the oven for 45 minutes, then turn the chicken over and baste with the juices. Cook for a further 45 minutes.

4 When the chicken is cooked, lift it to drain out any juices from the cavity into the pan, then transfer the bird to a warmed platter.

5 Place the roasting pan on the burner and heat until sizzling. Stir in the flour and cook for 1 minute, then stir in the cream, the remaining tarragon, ⅔ cup water, the lemon juice and seasoning. Boil and stir for 2–3 minutes, until thickened. Garnish the chicken with tarragon and lemon slices and serve with the sauce.

DUCK BREASTS WITH ORANGE SAUCE

A simple variation on the classic French whole roast duck.

Serves 4
4 duck breasts
1 tbsp sunflower oil
2 oranges
⅔ cup fresh orange juice
1 tbsp port
2 tbsp Seville orange marmalade
1 tbsp butter
1 tsp cornstarch
salt and black pepper

1 Season the duck breast skin. Heat the oil in a frying pan over a moderate heat and add the duck breasts, skin side down. Cover and cook for 3–4 minutes, until lightly browned. Turn the breasts over, lower the heat slightly and cook uncovered for 5–6 minutes.

2 Peel the skin and pith from the oranges. Working over a bowl to catch any juice, slice either side of the membranes to release the orange segments, then set aside with the juice.

3 Remove the duck breasts from the pan with a slotted spoon, drain on paper towel and keep warm in the oven while making the sauce. Drain off the fat from the pan.

4 Add the segmented oranges, all but 2 tbsp of the orange juice, the port and the orange marmalade to the pan. Bring to a boil and then reduce the heat slightly. Whisk small dabs of the butter into the sauce and season.

5 Blend the cornstarch with the reserved orange juice, pour into the pan and stir until slightly thickened. Add the duck breasts and cook gently for about 3 minutes. To serve, arrange the sliced breasts on plates with the sauce.

CRUMBED TURKEY STEAKS

The authentic Austrian recipe for *Weiner Schnitzel* uses veal escalopes (in fact the recipe originated from Milan in Italy, where Parmesan cheese replaced the bread crumbs.) Turkey breasts make a good alternative.

─────── INGREDIENTS ───────

Serves 4
4 turkey breast steaks (about 5oz each)
3 tbsp flour, seasoned
1 egg, lightly beaten
1½ cups fresh bread crumbs
5 tbsp finely grated Parmesan cheese
2 tbsp butter
3 tbsp sunflower oil
fresh parsley, to garnish
4 lemon wedges, to serve

1 Lay the turkey steaks between two sheets of plastic wrap. Pound each one with a rolling pin until flattened. Snip the edges of the steaks with scissors a few times to prevent them curling during cooking.

2 Place the seasoned flour on one plate, the egg into another and the bread crumbs and Parmesan mixed together on a third plate.

3 Dip each side of the steaks into the flour and shake off any excess. Next, dip them into the egg and then gently press each side into the bread crumbs and cheese until evenly coated.

4 Heat the butter and oil in a large frying pan and fry the turkey steaks on a moderate heat for 2–3 minutes on each side, until golden. Garnish with parsley and serve with lemon wedges.

COUNTRY CIDER HOT-POT

Game casseroles are popular all over the British Isles.

─────── INGREDIENTS ───────

Serves 4
2 tbsp flour
4 boneless rabbit pieces
2 tbsp butter
1 tbsp vegetable oil
15 baby onions
4 strips lean bacon, chopped
2 tsp Dijon mustard
1⅞ cups apple cider
3 carrots, chopped
2 parsnips, chopped
12 ready-to-eat prunes, pitted
1 fresh rosemary sprig
1 bay leaf
salt and black pepper

1 Preheat the oven to 325°F. Place the flour and seasoning in a plastic bag, add the rabbit pieces and shake until coated. Set aside.

2 Heat the butter and oil in a flame-proof casserole and add the onions and bacon. Fry for 4 minutes, until the onions have softened. Remove with a draining spoon and reserve.

3 Fry the seasoned rabbit pieces in the oil in the flameproof casserole until they are browned all over, then spread a little of the mustard over the top of each piece.

4 Return the onions and bacon to the pan. Pour on the cider and add the carrots, parsnips, prunes, rosemary and bay leaf. Season well. Bring to a boil, then cover and transfer to the oven. Cook for about 1½ hours until tender.

5 Remove the rosemary sprig and bay leaf and serve the rabbit hot with creamy mashed potatoes.

FISH AND SEAFOOD

There is nothing quite like the taste of freshly cooked fish and seafood. This chapter is packed with a host of recipes, from the simple to the sophisticated. There's no doubt that after tasting them you will find you could quite happily survive a meat shortage crisis! Try chunky Mediterranean Fish Stew topped with a pungent rouille sauce, Mussels with Wine and Garlic served with crusty French bread, or that great British favorite, Deep-Fried Spicy Smelts. Spanish Seafood Paella and Sizzling Chinese Steamed Fish are both dinner-party winners, while you can tempt the family with Tuna Fishcake Bites, Baked Fish Creole-Style, or Spaghetti with Seafood Sauce for supper.

MEDITERRANEAN FISH STEW

INGREDIENTS

Serves 4

2 cups cooked shrimp in shells
1lb mixed white fish fillets such as cod,
    whiting, haddock, mullet or monkfish
    skinned and chopped (reserve skins
    for the stock)
3 tbsp olive oil
1 onion, chopped
1 leek, sliced
1 carrot, diced
1 garlic clove, chopped
½ tsp ground turmeric
⅔ cup dry white wine or apple cider
14oz can chopped tomatoes
sprig each of fresh parsley, thyme
    and fennel
1 bay leaf
small piece of orange peel
1 cleaned squid, body cut into rings and
    tentacles chopped
12 mussels in shells
salt and black pepper
2–3 tbsp Parmesan cheese shavings,
    to sprinkle
chopped fresh parsley, to garnish

For the rouille sauce

2 slices white bread, crusts removed
2 garlic cloves, crushed
½ fresh red chili
1 tbsp tomato paste
3–4 tbsp olive oil

1 Peel the shrimp leaving the tails on; cover and chill. Place all the shrimp trimmings and fish trimmings in a pan and cover with 1⅞ cups water. Bring to a boil, then cover the pan and simmer for approximately 30 minutes. Strain and reserve the stock.

2 Heat the oil in a large saucepan and add the onion, leek, carrot and garlic. Fry gently for 6–7 minutes, then stir in the turmeric. Pour on the white wine, tomatoes and juice, the reserved fish stock, the herbs and orange peel. Bring to a boil, then cover and simmer gently for about 20 minutes.

3 Meanwhile, prepare the rouille sauce. Blend the bread in a food processor with the garlic, chili and tomato paste. With the motor running, pour in the oil in a thin drizzle until the mixture is smooth and thickened.

4 Add the fish and seafood to the pan and simmer for 5–6 minutes, or until the fish is opaque and the mussels are open. Remove the bay leaf and peel. Season the stew and serve in bowls with a spoonful of the rouille sauce, and sprinkled with Parmesan and parsley.

SCOTTISH SALMON WITH HERB BUTTER

INGREDIENTS

Serves 4

4 tbsp butter, softened
finely grated rind of ½ small lemon
1 tbsp lemon juice
1 tbsp chopped fresh dill
4 salmon steaks
2 lemon slices, halved
4 fresh dill sprigs
salt and black pepper

1 Place the butter, lemon rind, lemon juice, chopped dill and seasoning in a small bowl and mix together with a fork until blended.

2 Spoon the butter on to a piece of waxed paper and roll up, smoothing with your hands into a sausage shape. Twist the ends tightly, wrap in plastic wrap and pop in the freezer for 20 minutes, until firm.

COOK'S TIP
Other fresh herbs could be used to flavor the butter – try mint, fennel fronds, lemon balm, parsley or oregano instead of the dill.

3 Meanwhile, preheat the oven to 375°F. Cut out four squares of foil big enough to encase the salmon steaks and grease lightly. Place a salmon steak in the center of each one.

4 Remove the butter from the freezer and slice into eight rounds. Place two rounds on top of each salmon steak with a halved lemon slice in the center and a sprig of dill on top. Lift up the edges of the foil and crinkle them together until well sealed.

5 Lift the parcels on to a baking sheet and bake for about 20 minutes. Remove from the oven and place the unopened parcels on warmed plates. Open the parcels and slide the contents on to the plates with the juices.

CHINESE OMELETS WITH FRIED RICE

Makes 4

2 tbsp sesame oil
2 tbsp sesame seeds
1¼ cups cooked long grain rice
2in piece of cucumber, finely grated
1 tsp finely grated lemon rind
squeeze of lemon juice
6 eggs
1 tbsp dry sherry
1 tbsp light soy sauce
pinch of sugar
2 cups cooked, peeled shrimp
4 scallions, finely chopped
2 large tomatoes, seeded and chopped
2 tbsp vegetable oil
salt and black pepper
4 cooked shrimp in shells and fresh
   coriander sprigs, to garnish

1 Heat the sesame oil in a pan and fry the sesame seeds until golden. Stir in the cooked rice, followed by the cucumber, lemon rind and juice and seasoning. Cook for 2–3 minutes, then keep warm while making the omelets.

2 Place the eggs, sherry, soy sauce, sugar and a little pepper into a bowl and beat with a fork. Stir in the peeled shrimp, scallions and tomatoes.

3 Heat ½ tbsp of the oil in frying pan and ladle in a quarter of the mixture. Fry over a moderate heat for 3–4 minutes, until the omelet is lightly golden underneath. Cover and cook until the omelet is just set.

4 Remove the lid and fold the omelet in half. Garnish with a shrimp and fresh coriander and serve with a spoonful of the rice. Make the remaining omelets in the same way.

SIZZLING CHINESE STEAMED FISH

Steamed whole fish is very popular in China and the wok is used as a steamer. In this recipe the fish is flavored with garlic, ginger and scallions cooked in sizzling hot oil.

Serves 4

4 rainbow trout (about 9oz each)
¼ tsp salt
½ tsp sugar
2 garlic cloves, finely chopped
1 tbsp finely diced fresh ginger root
5 scallions, cut into 2in lengths and
   finely shredded
4 tbsp groundnut oil
1 tsp sesame oil
3 tbsp light soy sauce
thread egg noodles, to serve

1 Make three diagonal slits on both sides of each fish and lay them on a heatproof plate. Place a small rack or trivet in a wok or large frying pan half filled with water, cover and heat until just simmering.

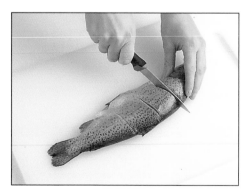

2 Sprinkle the fish with the salt, sugar, garlic and ginger. Sit the plate on the rack and cover. Steam gently for about 10–12 minutes, or until the flesh has turned pale pink and feels quite firm to the touch.

3 Turn off the heat, remove the lid and scatter the scallions over the fish. Replace the lid.

4 Heat the oils in a small pan over a high heat until just smoking, then quickly pour a quarter over the scallions on each of the fish – the shredded scallions will sizzle and cook in the hot oil – then sprinkle the soy sauce over the top. Serve the fish and juices immediately with boiled noodles.

SPANISH SEAFOOD PAELLA

───── INGREDIENTS ─────

Serves 4

4 tbsp olive oil

8oz monkfish or cod, skinned and cut into chunks

3 cleaned baby squid, body cut into rings and tentacles chopped

1 red mullet, filleted, skinned and cut into chunks (optional)

1 onion, chopped

3 garlic cloves, finely chopped

1 red bell pepper, seeded and sliced

4 tomatoes, skinned and chopped

1¼ cups arborio rice

1⅞ cups fish stock

⅔ cup white wine

¾ cup frozen peas

4–5 saffron strands soaked in 2 tbsp hot water

1 cup cooked, peeled shrimp

8 fresh mussels in shells, scrubbed

salt and black pepper

1 tbsp chopped fresh parsley, to garnish

lemon wedges, to serve

1 Heat 2 tbsp of the oil in a large frying pan and add the monkfish or cod, the squid and the red mullet, if using, to the pan. Stir-fry for 2 minutes, then transfer the fish to a bowl with all the juices and reserve.

2 Heat the remaining 2 tbsp of oil in the pan and add the onion, garlic and pepper. Fry for 6–7 minutes, stirring frequently, until the onion and pepper have softened.

3 Stir in the tomatoes and fry for 2 minutes, then add the rice, stirring to coat the grains with oil, and cook for 2–3 minutes. Pour on the fish stock and wine and add the peas, saffron and water. Season well and mix.

4 Gently stir in the reserved cooked fish with all the juices, followed by the shrimp; and then push the mussels into the rice. Cover and cook over a gentle heat for about 30 minutes, or until the stock has been absorbed but the mixture is still moist.

5 Remove from the heat, keep covered and leave to stand for 5 minutes. Sprinkle with parsley and serve with lemon wedges.

SPAGHETTI WITH SEAFOOD SAUCE

The Italian name for this tomato-based sauce is *marinara*.

INGREDIENTS

Serves 4
3 tbsp olive oil
1 medium onion, chopped
1 garlic clove, finely chopped
8oz spaghetti
2½ cups crushed tomatoes
1 tbsp tomato paste
1 tsp dried oregano
1 bay leaf
1 tsp sugar
1 cup cooked, peeled baby shrimp
  (rinsed well if canned)
1 cup cooked, peeled large shrimp
1½ cups cooked clams or mussels
  (rinsed well if canned or bottled)
1 tbsp lemon juice
3 tbsp chopped fresh parsley
2 tbsp butter
salt and black pepper
4 whole cooked large shrimp,
  to garnish

1 Heat the oil in a pan and add the onion and garlic. Fry over a moderate heat for 6–7 minutes, until the onion has softened.

2 Meanwhile, cook the spaghetti in a large pan of boiling salted water for 10–12 minutes until *al dente*.

3 Stir the crushed tomatoes, paste, oregano, bay leaf and sugar into the onions and season well. Bring to a boil, then simmer for 2–3 minutes.

4 Add the shellfish, lemon juice and 2 tbsp of the parsley. Stir well, then cover and cook for 3–5 minutes.

5 Meanwhile, drain the spaghetti when it is ready and add the butter to the pan. Return the drained spaghetti to the pan and toss in the butter. Season well.

6 Divide the spaghetti among four warmed plates and top with the seafood sauce. Sprinkle with the remaining 1 tbsp chopped parsley, garnish with whole shrimp and then serve immediately.

DEEP-FRIED SPICY SMELTS

A delicious British dish – serve these tiny fish very hot and crisp.

INGREDIENTS

Serves 4
1lb smelts
3 tbsp flour
1 tsp paprika
pinch of cayenne pepper
12 fresh parsley sprigs
vegetable oil, for deep-frying
salt and black pepper
4 lemon wedges, to garnish

1 If using frozen smelts, defrost in the bag and drain off any water. Spread the fish on paper towel and pat dry.

2 Place the flour, paprika, cayenne and seasoning into a large plastic bag. Add the smelts and shake gently until all the fish are lightly coated with the flour. Transfer to a plate.

3 Heat about 2in of oil in a pan or deep-fat fryer to 375°F, or until a cube of bread dropped in browns in 30 seconds.

4 Add the smelts in batches and deep-fry in the hot oil for 2–3 minutes, until the coating is lightly golden and crispy. Remove, drain on paper towel and keep warm in the oven while frying the remainder.

5 When all the smelts are cooked, drop the sprigs of parsley into the hot oil (don't worry if the oil spits a bit) and fry for a few seconds until crisp. Drain on paper towel. Serve the smelts garnished with the deep-fried parsley sprigs and lemon wedges.

PORTUGUESE GRILLED SARDINES

INGREDIENTS

Serves 4
8–12 fresh sardines (depending on size)
5 tbsp olive oil
juice of 1 lemon
1 tsp finely grated lemon rind
2 tbsp chopped fresh parsley
salt and black pepper
4 lemon wedges, tomato salad and hot garlic bread, to serve

1 First of all, remove the scales by holding the fish by their tails under running water and gently rubbing the skin with your fingers from the tail towards the head. Make a slit in the belly and remove the innards, rinse the fish and pat dry with paper towel. Make two diagonal slashes in the skin on both sides of each sardine and transfer to a plate.

2 Preheat the broiler. Mix together the oil, lemon juice, lemon rind, parsley and seasoning. Brush the fish with the marinade and place on a broiling rack.

3 Cook under a moderate heat for about 2–3 minutes, basting once, until the skin is starting to crispen and then carefully turn the fish over. Brush with some more of the marinade. Broil for a further 2–3 minutes.

4 Lift the sardines carefully on to a warmed serving platter and pour over the remaining marinade. Serve with lemon wedges, a tomato salad and hot crusty garlic bread.

> COOK'S TIP
> Sardines are baby pilchards and can be rather bony – so beware. Always choose firm, fresh fish. Bright eyes are a sign of freshness.

BAKED FISH CREOLE-STYLE

INGREDIENTS

Serves 4

1 tbsp vegetable oil
2 tbsp butter
1 onion, thinly sliced
1 garlic clove, chopped
1 red bell pepper, seeded, halved
   and sliced
1 green bell pepper, seeded, halved
   and sliced
14oz can chopped tomatoes with basil
1 tbsp tomato paste
2 tbsp chopped capers
3–4 drops Tabasco sauce
4 tail end pieces cod or haddock fillets
   (about 6oz each), skinned
6 basil leaves, shredded
3 tbsp fresh bread crumbs
¼ cup grated Cheddar cheese
2 tsp chopped fresh parsley
salt and black pepper
fresh basil sprigs, to garnish

1 Preheat the oven to 450°F. Grease an ovenproof dish.

2 Heat the oil and half the butter in a pan and add the onion. Fry for about 6–7 minutes, until softened, then add the garlic, peppers, chopped tomatoes, tomato paste, capers and Tabasco and season well. Cover and cook for 15 minutes, then uncover and simmer gently for 5 minutes to reduce slightly.

3 Place the fish fillets in the ovenproof dish, dot with the remaining 1 tbsp butter and season lightly. Spoon over the tomato and pepper sauce and sprinkle over the shredded basil. Bake in the oven for about 10 minutes.

4 Meanwhile, mix together the bread crumbs, cheese and parsley in a bowl.

5 Remove the fish from the oven and scatter the cheese and bread crumbs over the top. Return to the oven and bake for a further 10 minutes, until lightly browned.

6 Let the fish stand for about a minute, then, using a spatula, carefully transfer each topped fillet to warmed plates. Garnish with sprigs of fresh basil and serve hot.

TUNA FISHCAKE BITES

An updated version of a traditional British tea-time dish.

INGREDIENTS

Serves 4
1½lb (about 5 medium) potatoes
1½ tbsp butter
2 hard-boiled eggs, chopped
3 scallions, finely chopped
finely grated rind of ½ lemon
1 tsp lemon juice
2 tbsp chopped fresh parsley
7oz can tuna in oil, drained
2 tsp capers, chopped
2 eggs, lightly beaten
2 cups fresh white bread crumbs,
    for coating
sunflower oil, for frying
salt and black pepper
mixed salad, to serve

For the tartar sauce
4 tbsp mayonnaise
1 tbsp natural yogurt
1 tbsp finely chopped gherkins
1 tbsp chopped capers
1 tbsp chopped fresh parsley

1 Cook the potatoes in a pot of boiling salted water until tender. Drain well, add the butter and mash well. Leave to cool.

2 Add the hard-boiled eggs, scallions, lemon rind, lemon juice, parsley, tuna, capers and 1 tbsp of the beaten egg to the cooled potato. Mix well with a fork and season. Cover and chill for about 30 minutes.

3 Meanwhile, place all the ingredients for the tartar sauce in a bowl and mix well. Chill and reserve.

4 Pour the remaining beaten egg into one shallow bowl and the bread crumbs into another. Roll the chilled fishcake mixture into about 24 balls. Dip these into the egg and then roll gently in the bread crumbs until evenly coated. Transfer to a plate.

5 Heat 6 tbsp of oil in a frying pan and fry the balls on a moderate heat, in batches, for about 4 minutes, turning two or three times until they are browned all over. Drain on paper towel and keep warm in the oven while frying the remainder.

6 Serve about six balls per person with the tartar sauce and a salad.

KASHMIR COCONUT FISH CURRY

INGREDIENTS

Serves 4

2 tbsp vegetable oil
2 onions, sliced
1 green bell pepper, seeded and sliced
1 garlic clove, crushed
1 dried chili, seeded and chopped
1 tsp ground coriander
1 tsp ground cumin
½ tsp ground turmeric
½ tsp hot chili powder
½ tsp garam masala
1 tbsp flour
4oz creamed coconut, chopped
1½lb haddock fillets, skinned
  and chopped
4 tomatoes, skinned, seeded
  and chopped
1 tbsp lemon juice
2 tbsp ground almonds
2 tbsp heavy cream
fresh coriander sprigs, to garnish
naan bread and boiled rice, to serve

1 Heat the oil in a large saucepan and add the onions, pepper and garlic. Cook for 6–7 minutes, until the onions and pepper have softened. Stir in the chopped dried chili, all the ground spices, the chili powder, garam masala and flour, and cook for 1 minute.

2 Dissolve the coconut in 2½ cups boiling water and stir into the spicy vegetable mixture. Bring to a boil, cover and then simmer gently for about 6 minutes.

3 Add the fish and tomatoes and cook for about 5–6 minutes, or until the fish has turned opaque. Uncover and gently stir in the lemon juice, ground almonds and cream. Season well, garnish with coriander and serve with naan bread and rice.

COOK'S TIP
Replace the haddock with any firm fleshed white fish such as cod or whiting. Stir in a few cooked, peeled shrimp, if you like.

MUSSELS WITH WINE AND GARLIC

This famous French dish is traditionally known as *Moules Marinières*.

INGREDIENTS

Serves 4

4lb (about 4 pints) fresh
  mussels in shells
1 tbsp oil
2 tbsp butter
1 small onion or 2 shallots, finely
  chopped
2 garlic cloves, finely chopped
⅔ cup dry white wine or
  apple cider
fresh parsley sprigs
black pepper
2 tbsp chopped fresh parsley,
  to garnish
French bread, to serve

1 Check that the mussels are closed. (Throw away any that are cracked or won't close when tapped.) Scrape the shells under cold running water and pull off the hairy beards attached to the hinges of the shells. Rinse well in two or three changes of water.

2 Heat the oil and butter in a large pan, add the onion or shallots and garlic and fry for 3–4 minutes.

3 Pour on the wine or cider and add the parsley sprigs. Stir well, bring to the boil, then add the mussels. Cover and cook for about 5–7 minutes, shaking the pan once or twice until the shells open (throw away any that have not).

4 Serve the mussels and their juices sprinkled with the chopped parsley and a few grinds of black pepper. Accompany with hot French bread.

THAI SHRIMP SALAD

This salad has the distinctive flavour of lemon grass, the bulbous grass used widely in South-east Asian cooking.

INGREDIENTS

Serves 4 as an appetizer
9oz cooked, peeled extra large
*   tiger shrimp*
1 tbsp oriental fish sauce
2 tbsp lime juice
½ tsp soft light brown sugar
1 small fresh red chili, finely chopped
1 scallion, finely chopped
1 small garlic clove, crushed
1in piece fresh lemon grass,
*   finely chopped*
2 tbsp chopped fresh coriander
3 tbsp dry white wine
8–12 Boston lettuce leaves, to serve
fresh coriander sprigs, to garnish

1 Place the tiger shrimp in a bowl and add all the remaining ingredients. Stir well, cover and leave to marinate in the fridge for 2–3 hours, mixing and turning the shrimp occasionally.

2 Arrange two or three of the lettuce leaves on each of four individual serving plates.

3 Spoon the shrimp salad into the lettuce leaves. Garnish with fresh coriander and serve at once.

COOK'S TIP
If you find raw shrimp, cook them in boiling water until pink and use instead of the cooked shrimp.

CAJUN SPICED FISH

Cajun blackened fish is a speciality of Paul Prudhommes, a chef from New Orleans. Fillets of fish are coated with an aromatic blend of herbs and spices and pan-fried in butter.

INGREDIENTS

Serves 4
1 tsp dried thyme
1 tsp dried oregano
1 tsp ground black pepper
¼ tsp cayenne pepper
2 tsp paprika
½ tsp garlic salt
4 tail end pieces of cod fillet
*   (about 6oz each)*
6 tbsp butter
½ red bell pepper, sliced
½ green bell pepper, sliced
fresh thyme, to garnish
broiled tomatoes and sweet potato
*   purée, to serve*

1 Place all the herbs and spices in a bowl and mix well. Dip the fish fillets in the spice mixture until lightly coated.

2 Heat 2 tbsp of the butter in a large frying pan, add the peppers and fry for 4–5 minutes, until softened. Remove the peppers and keep warm.

3 Add the remaining butter to the pan and heat until sizzling. Add the cod fillets and fry on a moderate heat for 3–4 minutes on each side, until they are browned and cooked.

4 Transfer the fish to a warmed serving dish, surround with the peppers and garnish with thyme. Serve the spiced fish with some broiled tomatoes and sweet potato purée.

COOK'S TIP
This blend of herbs and spices can be used to flavor any fish steaks or fillets and could also be used to jazz up pan-fried shrimp.

PASTA, PIZZAS AND GRAINS

This chapter is full of recipes that will bring back memories of sunshine vacations all over the world. From Italy comes a favorite recipe for Spinach and Cheese Dumplings drenched in a lemon and basil butter, as well as a classic creamy Asparagus and Cheese Risotto, and a Roman recipe for Pasta Carbonara. For pizza lovers there is a thick-crusted variety packed with spicy pepperoni and sweet peppers, and a French Onion Tart from the heart of Provence. For a cold meal, the Middle Eastern Lemony Bulgar Wheat Salad is easy and delicious. From Morocco, steamed couscous topped with honeyed chicken makes the ideal dinner-party dish. For speedy stir-fried meals, go for the Far Eastern Thai Fried Noodles, and Chinese Special Fried Rice – versatile recipes where the ingredients are infinitely variable.

PEPPERONI PIZZA

INGREDIENTS

Makes a 12in pizza

For the sauce

2 tbsp olive oil
1 onion, finely chopped
1 garlic clove, crushed
14oz can chopped tomatoes
   with herbs
1 tbsp tomato paste

For the pizza base

2½ cups flour
½ tsp salt
1 tsp fast-rising yeast
2 tbsp olive oil

For the topping

½ red bell pepper, sliced into rings
½ yellow bell pepper, sliced into rings
½ green bell pepper, sliced into rings
5oz mozzarella cheese, sliced
½ cup pepperoni sausage,
   thinly sliced
8 black olives, pitted
3 sun-dried tomatoes in oil, chopped
½ tsp dried oregano
olive oil, for drizzling

1 To make the sauce, heat the oil in a pan and then add the onion and garlic. Fry gently for about 6–7 minutes, until softened. Add the tomatoes and stir in the tomato paste. Bring to a boil and boil rapidly for 5 minutes, until reduced slightly. Remove the pan from the heat and leave to cool.

2 For the pizza base, lightly grease a 12in round pizza tray. Sift the flour and salt into a bowl. Sprinkle over the fast-rising yeast and make a well in the center. Pour in about ¾ cup warm water and the olive oil, and then mix to a soft dough.

3 Place the dough on a lightly floured surface and knead for about 5–10 minutes, until smooth. Roll out to a 10in round, making the edges slightly thicker than the center. Lift the dough on to the pizza tray.

4 Spread the tomato sauce over the dough and then top with the peppers, mozzarella, pepperoni sausage, black olives and tomatoes. Sprinkle over the oregano and drizzle with olive oil. Cover loosely and leave in a warm place for 30 minutes, until slightly risen. In the meantime, preheat the oven to 425°F.

5 Bake for 25–30 minutes and serve hot straight from the tray.

BROCCOLI AND RICOTTA CANNELLONI

INGREDIENTS

Serves 4

12 dried cannelloni tubes, about
    3in long
4 cups broccoli florets
1½ cups fresh bread crumbs
⅔ cup milk
4 tbsp extra virgin olive oil, plus
    extra for brushing
1 cup ricotta cheese
pinch of grated nutmeg
6 tbsp finely grated Parmesan or
    Pecorino cheese
salt and black pepper
2 tbsp pine nuts, for sprinkling

For the tomato sauce
2 tbsp olive oil
1 onion, finely chopped
1 garlic clove, crushed
2 x 14oz cans chopped tomatoes
1 tbsp tomato paste
4 black olives, pitted and chopped
1 tsp dried thyme

1 Preheat the oven to 375°F and lightly grease an ovenproof dish with olive oil. Bring a large pot of water to a boil, add a little of the olive oil and simmer the cannelloni, uncovered, for approximately 6–7 minutes, or until it is nearly cooked.

2 Meanwhile, steam or boil the broccoli for 10 minutes, until tender. Drain the pasta, rinse under cold water and reserve. Drain the broccoli and leave to cool, then place in a food processor or blender, whizz until smooth and set aside.

3 Place the bread crumbs in a bowl, add the milk and oil and stir until softened. Add the ricotta, broccoli purée, nutmeg, 4 tbsp of the Parmesan cheese and seasoning, then set aside.

4 To make the sauce, heat the oil in a frying pan and add the onion and garlic. Fry for 5–6 minutes, until softened, then stir in the tomatoes, tomato paste, black olives, thyme and seasoning. Boil rapidly for 2–3 minutes, then pour into the base of the dish.

5 Spoon the cheese mixture into a piping bag fitted with a ½in nozzle. Carefully open the cannelloni tubes. Standing each one upright on a board, pipe the filling into each tube. Lay them in rows in the tomato sauce.

6 Brush the tops of the cannelloni with a little olive oil and sprinkle over the remaining Parmesan cheese and pine nuts. Bake in the oven for about 25–30 minutes, until golden on top.

ITALIAN PASTA WITH PESTO SAUCE

Serves 4
a little olive oil
12oz fresh paglia e fieno *pasta*
4 sun-dried tomatoes in oil, chopped
Parmesan cheese shavings (made using
  a potato peeler) and fresh basil sprigs,
  to garnish
French bread, to serve

For the pesto
¼ cup pine nuts
2 cups fresh parsley sprigs
2 cups fresh basil leaves
2 garlic cloves, chopped
¾ cup olive oil
6 tbsp finely grated Pecorino or
  Parmesan cheese
salt and black pepper

1 To make the pesto, place the pine nuts in a small frying pan and dry-fry until lightly browned all over. When cooled, place in a food processor or blender with the parsley, basil and garlic and pulse until finely chopped.

2 With the motor running, slowly pour on the olive oil in a thin stream and the mixture will thicken.

3 Finally, add the grated cheese and pulse for a few short bursts until well mixed in. Season and set aside.

4 Bring a large pot of salted water to a boil and add a little olive oil. Add the fresh pasta and cook for 3–4 minutes, until *al dente*. Drain well and return to the pot.

5 Stir in the pesto sauce and mix well until all the pasta is thoroughly coated. Divide between warmed individual serving bowls and top with chopped sun-dried tomatoes, Parmesan cheese shavings and a sprig of fresh basil. Serve with hot French bread.

FRENCH ONION TART

Serves 6
2 tbsp olive oil
6 medium onions, thinly sliced
2 garlic cloves, crushed

For the dough
10oz package pizza base mix
1 tsp olive oil
2oz can (about 12) anchovy fillets,
  sliced in half lengthwise
8 black olives, pitted
2 tsp chopped fresh thyme, or ½ tsp
  dried thyme
salt and black pepper

1 Heat the oil in a frying pan, add the sliced onions and garlic and season lightly. Fry gently, stirring occasionally, for about 40 minutes, or until the onions are soft but not too brown.

2 Preheat the oven to 425°F. Empty the pizza base mix into a bowl, stir in 1 cup warm water and add the oil. Mix to a dough and then knead for about 5 minutes.

3 Lightly grease a 13 x 9in jelly roll pan. Roll out the dough on a lightly floured surface to fit the pan and press into the base. Spread the cooked onions evenly over the dough base and then arrange the anchovy fillets on top in a lattice pattern.

4 Scatter over the olives and chopped thyme and drizzle with a little more olive oil. Place in a large sealed plastic bag and leave to rise in a warm place for 15 minutes.

5 Bake for 10 minutes, then reduce the temperature to 375°F and cook for 15–20 minutes, or until golden brown around the edges. Cut into six pieces and serve warm or cold.

Asparagus and Cheese Risotto

An authentic Italian risotto has a unique creamy texture achieved by constant stirring of the arborio rice, available from supermarkets or gourmet stores.

Ingredients

Serves 4

¼ tsp saffron strands
about 2½ cups hot chicken stock
2 tbsp butter
2 tbsp olive oil
1 large onion, finely chopped
2 garlic cloves, finely chopped
1¼ cups arborio rice
1¼ cups dry white wine
8oz asparagus tips (or asparagus cut
  into 2in lengths), cooked
1 cup finely grated Parmesan cheese
salt and black pepper
Parmesan shavings and fresh basil
  sprigs, to garnish
ciabatta bread rolls and salad, to serve

1 Sprinkle the saffron over the stock and leave to stand for 5 minutes.

2 Heat the butter and oil in a frying pan and add the onion and garlic. Fry for 6 minutes, until softened.

3 Add the rice and stir-fry for 1–2 minutes to coat the grains with the butter and oil.

4 Pour on 1¼ cups of the hot chicken stock and saffron mixture. Cook gently over a moderate heat, stirring frequently, until almost all the liquid has been absorbed.

5 Repeat with another 1¼ cups stock. When that has been absorbed, add the wine and carry on cooking and stirring frequently until the rice has a creamy consistency.

6 Add the asparagus and remaining stock and stir until the liquid is absorbed and the rice is tender. Stir in the Parmesan cheese and season well.

7 Spoon the risotto on to warmed plates and garnish with the Parmesan cheese shavings and fresh basil. Serve with hot ciabatta rolls and a crisp green salad.

MOROCCAN CHICKEN COUSCOUS

Serves 4

1 tbsp butter
1 tbsp sunflower oil
4 chicken pieces
2 onions, finely chopped
2 garlic cloves, crushed
½ tsp ground cinnamon
¼ tsp ground ginger
¼ tsp ground turmeric
2 tbsp orange juice
2 tsp honey
salt and black pepper
fresh mint sprigs, to garnish

For the couscous

2¼ cups couscous
1 tsp salt
2 tsp sugar
2 tbsp sunflower oil
½ tsp ground cinnamon
pinch of grated nutmeg
1 tbsp orange blossom water
2 tbsp sultanas
½ cup chopped blanched almonds
3 tbsp chopped pistachio nuts

1 Heat the butter and oil in a large pan and add the chicken pieces, skin side down. Fry for 3–4 minutes, until the skin is golden, then turn over.

2 Add the onions, garlic, spices and a pinch of salt and pour over the orange juice and 1¼ cups water. Cover the pan and bring to a boil, then reduce the heat and simmer for about 30 minutes.

3 Meanwhile, place the couscous and salt in a bowl and cover with 1½ cups water. Stir once and leave the couscous to stand for 5 minutes. Add the sugar, 1 tbsp of the oil, the cinnamon, nutmeg, orange blossom water and sultanas to the couscous and mix very well.

4 Heat the remaining 1 tbsp of the oil in a pan and lightly fry the almonds until golden. Stir into the couscous with the pistachio nuts.

5 Line a steamer with parchment paper and spoon in the couscous. Sit the steamer over the chicken (or over a pan of boiling water) and steam for 10 minutes.

6 Remove the steamer and keep covered. Stir the honey into the chicken liquid and boil rapidly for 3–4 minutes. Spoon the couscous on to a warmed serving platter and top with the chicken, with a little of the sauce spooned over. Garnish with mint sprigs and serve with the remaining sauce.

PASTA CARBONARA

An Italian favorite and a classic Roman dish, whose name translates as "charcoal burners' pasta." Traditionally made with spaghetti, it is equally delicious with fresh egg tagliatelle.

INGREDIENTS

Serves 4
12oz–1lb fresh tagliatelle
1 tbsp olive oil
8oz piece of ham, bacon or pancetta,
  cut into 1in sticks
4oz (about 10) button mushrooms,
  thinly sliced
4 eggs, lightly beaten
5 tbsp light cream
2 tbsp finely grated Parmesan cheese
salt and black pepper
fresh basil sprigs, to garnish

1 Cook the pasta in a pot of boiling salted water, with a little oil added, for 3–4 minutes or until *al dente*.

2 Meanwhile, heat the oil in a frying pan and add the ham, bacon or pancetta. Fry for 3–4 minutes, add the mushrooms and fry for a further 3–4 minutes. Turn off the heat and reserve. Lightly beat the eggs and cream together in a bowl and season well.

3 Drain the cooked pasta and return it to the pan. Add the ham, bacon or pancetta, the mushrooms and any pan juices and stir into the pasta.

4 Pour in the eggs and cream and half the Parmesan cheese. Stir well and as you do this the eggs will cook in the heat of the pasta. Pile on to warmed serving plates, sprinkle with the remaining Parmesan and garnish with basil.

BAKED MACARONI AND CHEESE

A classic American supper – replace the Cheddar with your family's favorite cheese.

INGREDIENTS

Serves 4
1 tbsp olive oil
2⅓ cups short cut macaroni
2 leeks, chopped
4 tbsp butter
½ cup flour
3¾ cups milk
2 cups grated sharp Cheddar cheese
2 tbsp ricotta cheese
1 tsp whole grain mustard
1 cup fresh bread crumbs
½ cup grated Double Gloucester cheese
salt and black pepper
1 tbsp chopped fresh parsley,
  to garnish

1 Preheat the oven to 350°F. Bring a large pot of salted water to a boil and pour in the olive oil. Add the macaroni and leeks and boil gently for 10 minutes. Drain, rinse under cold water and reserve.

2 Heat the butter in a saucepan, stir in the flour and cook for about a minute. Remove from the heat and gradually add the milk, stirring well after each addition until smooth. Return to the heat and stir continuously until thickened.

3 Add the Cheddar cheese, ricotta cheese and mustard, mix well, and season with salt and pepper.

4 Stir the drained macaroni and leeks into the cheese sauce and pile into a greased ovenproof dish. Level the top with the back of a spoon and sprinkle over the bread crumbs and Double Gloucester cheese.

5 Bake for 35–40 minutes. Serve hot, garnished with fresh parsley.

LOUISIANA RICE

Serves 4

4 tbsp vegetable oil
1 small eggplant, diced
8oz ground pork
1 green bell pepper, seeded and chopped
2 stalks celery, chopped
1 onion, chopped
1 garlic clove, crushed
1 tsp cayenne pepper
1 tsp paprika
1 tsp black pepper
½ tsp salt
1 tsp dried thyme
½ tsp dried oregano
2 cups chicken stock
8oz chicken livers, finely chopped
¾ cup long grain rice
1 bay leaf
3 tbsp chopped fresh parsley
celery leaves, to garnish

3 Add the pepper, celery, onion, garlic and all the spices and herbs. Cover and cook on a high heat for 5–6 minutes, stirring frequently from the bottom to scrape up and distribute the crispy brown bits.

4 Pour on the chicken stock and stir to clean the bottom of the pan. Cover and cook for 6 minutes over a moderate heat. Stir in the chicken livers, cook for 2 minutes, then mix in the rice and add the bay leaf.

2 Add the pork and cook for about 6–8 minutes, until browned, using a wooden spoon to break any lumps.

1 Heat the oil in a frying pan until really hot, then add the eggplant and stir-fry for about 5 minutes.

5 Reduce the heat, cover and simmer for about 6–7 minutes. Turn off the heat and leave to stand for a further 10–15 minutes until the rice is tender. Remove the bay leaf and stir in the chopped parsley. Serve the rice hot, garnished with the celery leaves.

SPINACH AND CHEESE DUMPLINGS

These little dumplings are known as *gnocchi* in Italy.

INGREDIENTS

Serves 4

1¼ *cups cold mashed potato*
½ *cup semolina*
1 *cup frozen leaf spinach, defrosted,*
   squeezed and chopped
½ *cup ricotta cheese*
5 *tbsp grated Parmesan cheese, plus*
   2tbsp for sprinkling
2 *tbsp beaten egg*
½ *tsp salt*
large pinch of grated nutmeg
black pepper
fresh basil sprigs, to garnish

For the butter

6 *tbsp butter*
1 *tsp grated lemon rind*
1 *tbsp lemon juice*
1 *tbsp chopped fresh basil*

1 Place all the gnocchi ingredients except the basil in a bowl and mix well. Take small pieces of the mixture, about the size of a walnut, and roll each one back and forth a few times along the prongs of a fork until ridged. Repeat until you have 28 gnocchi and lay on a tray lined with plastic wrap.

2 Bring a large pot of water to the boil, reduce the heat slightly, and drop the gnocchi into the simmering water. They will sink to the bottom at first, but as they cook they will rise to the surface – this will take about 2 minutes, then simmer for about 1 minute.

3 Remove the gnocchi with a slotted spoon and transfer to a lightly greased and warmed ovenproof dish.

4 Sprinkle the gnocchi with a little Parmesan cheese and broil under a high heat for about 2 minutes, or until lightly browned. Meanwhile, heat the butter in a pan and stir in the lemon rind and juice, basil and seasoning.

5 Pour a quarter of the hot butter over each portion of gnocchi and garnish with fresh basil. Serve hot.

CHINESE SPECIAL FRIED RICE

Cooked white rice fried with a selection of other ingredients is a staple Chinese dish. This recipe combines a mixture of chicken, shrimp and vegetables with the fried rice.

INGREDIENTS

Serves 4
1 cup long grain white rice
3 tbsp groundnut oil
1 garlic clove, crushed
4 scallions, finely chopped
1 cup diced cooked chicken
1 cup cooked, peeled shrimp (rinsed if canned)
½ cup frozen peas
1 egg, beaten with a pinch of salt
1 cup shredded, lettuce
2 tbsp light soy sauce
pinch of sugar
salt and black pepper
1 tbsp chopped, roasted cashew nuts, to garnish

1 Rinse the rice in two to three changes of warm water to wash away some of the starch. Drain well.

2 Put the rice in a saucepan and add 1 tbsp of the oil and 1½ cups water. Cover and bring to a boil, stir once, then cover and simmer for 12–15 minutes, until nearly all the water has been absorbed. Turn off the heat and leave, covered, to stand for 10 minutes. Fluff up with a fork and leave to cool.

3 Heat the remaining oil in a wok or frying pan, add the garlic and scallions and stir-fry for 30 seconds.

4 Add the chicken, shrimp and peas and stir-fry for 1–2 minutes, then add the cooked rice and stir-fry for a further 2 minutes. Pour in the egg and stir-fry until just set. Stir in the lettuce, soy sauce, sugar and seasoning.

5 Transfer to a warmed serving bowl, sprinkle with the chopped cashew nuts and serve immediately.

LEMONY BULGUR WHEAT SALAD

This nutty Middle Eastern salad called *Tabbouleh* is delicious as an accompaniment to grilled meats or fish or on its own.

INGREDIENTS

Serves 4
1½ cups bulgur wheat
4 scallions, finely chopped
5 tbsp chopped fresh mint
5 tbsp chopped fresh parsley
1 tbsp chopped fresh coriander
2 medium tomatoes, skinned and chopped
juice of 1 lemon
5 tbsp olive oil
salt and black pepper
fresh mint sprigs, to garnish

1 Place the bulgur wheat in a bowl, pour on enough boiling water to cover and leave to soak for 20 minutes.

2 After soaking, place the bulgur wheat in a large sieve and drain thoroughly. Transfer to a bowl.

3 Stir in the chopped scallions, herbs, tomatoes, lemon juice, olive oil and seasoning. Mix well and chill for about an hour. Garnish with mint sprigs.

INDIAN PILAU RICE

INGREDIENTS

Serves 4

1¼ cups basmati rice, well rinsed
1 small onion, finely chopped
1 garlic clove, crushed
2 tbsp vegetable oil
1 tsp fennel seeds
1 tbsp sesame seeds
½ tsp ground turmeric
1 tsp ground cumin
¼ tsp salt
2 whole cloves
4 cardamom pods, lightly crushed
5 black peppercorns
1⅞ cups chicken stock
1 tbsp ground almonds
fresh coriander sprigs, to garnish

1 Soak the rice in water for 30 minutes. Heat the oil in a pan, add the onion and garlic, and fry gently for 5–6 minutes, until softened.

2 Stir in the fennel and sesame seeds, the turmeric, cumin, salt, cloves, cardamom pods and peppercorns and fry for about a minute. Drain the rice well, add to the pan and stir-fry for a further 3 minutes.

3 Pour on the chicken stock. Bring to a boil, then cover, reduce the heat to very low and simmer gently for 20 minutes, without removing the lid, until all the liquid has been absorbed.

4 Remove from the heat and leave to stand for 2–3 minutes. Fork up the rice and stir in the ground almonds. Garnish with coriander sprigs.

THAI FRIED NOODLES

INGREDIENTS

Serves 4

8oz thread egg noodles
4 tbsp vegetable oil
2 garlic cloves, finely chopped
6oz pork tenderloin, sliced into
   thin strips
1 boneless, skinless chicken breast
   (about 6oz), sliced into thin strips
1 cup cooked, peeled shrimp
   (rinsed if canned)
3 tbsp lime or lemon juice
3 tbsp oriental fish sauce
2 tbsp soft light brown sugar
2 eggs, beaten
½ red chili, seeded and finely chopped
¾ cup beansprouts
4 tbsp roasted peanuts, chopped
3 scallions, cut into 2in lengths
   and shredded
3 tbsp chopped fresh coriander

1 Place the noodles in a large pan of boiling water and leave to stand for about 5 minutes.

2 Meanwhile, heat 3 tbsp of the oil in a wok or large frying pan, add the garlic and cook for 30 seconds. Add the pork and chicken and stir-fry on a high heat until lightly browned, then add the shrimp and stir-fry for 2 minutes.

3 Add the lime or lemon juice, fish sauce and sugar and stir-fry until the sugar has dissolved.

4 Drain the noodles and add to the pan with the remaining 1 tbsp oil. Toss all the ingredients together.

5 Pour on the beaten eggs. Stir-fry until almost set, then add the chili and beansprouts. Divide the peanuts, scallions and coriander leaves into two and add half to the pan. Stir-fry for 2 minutes, then tip on to a serving platter. Sprinkle on the remaining peanuts, scallions and coriander and serve at once.

VEGETABLES AND SALADS

Nowadays, vegetables are taking center-stage on menus all over the world, and this chapter demonstrates just how versatile and delicious they can be. The hearty Salade Niçoise, delicious Ratatouille stewed in fruity olive oil, and Mixed Pepper Salad are all from the shores of the Mediterranean. From the Far East, Chinese Crispy Seaweed topped with sweetened almonds is easy to make, and from America hails the crunchy Caesar Salad, packed with crisp croûtons and garlic. Add a touch of zing to potatoes – serve Bombay Spiced Potatoes, or the fiery Spanish Chili Potatoes – or, if you have a sweeter tooth, try Candied Sweet Potatoes with Bacon. For the ideal accompaniment to a main course, choose from delicious, creamy Leek and Parsnip Purée, Mexican Re-Fried Beans, and Chinese Vegetable Stir-Fry.

SALADE NIÇOISE

INGREDIENTS

Serves 4

6 tbsp olive oil
2 tbsp tarragon vinegar
1 tsp tarragon or Dijon mustard
1 small garlic clove, crushed
1 cup green beans
12 small new or salad potatoes
3–4 Boston lettuces, roughly chopped
7oz can tuna in oil, drained
6 anchovy fillets, halved lengthwise
12 black olives, pitted
4 tomatoes, chopped
4 scallions, finely chopped
2 tsp capers
2 tbsp pine nuts
2 hard-boiled eggs, chopped
salt and black pepper
crusty bread, to serve

1 Mix the oil, vinegar, mustard, garlic and seasoning with a wooden spoon in the base of a large salad bowl.

2 Cook the green beans and the potatoes in separate pans of boiling salted water until just tender. Drain and add to the bowl with the lettuce, tuna, anchovies, olives, tomatoes, scallions and capers.

3 Just before serving toast the pine nuts in a small frying pan until lightly browned.

4 Sprinkle over the salad while still hot, add the eggs and toss all the ingredients together well. Serve with chunks of hot crusty bread.

COOK'S TIP
Look out for delicious salad potatoes like fingerling, Yukon Gold or Peruvian blue potatoes for an exotic and flavorful twist.

CAESAR SALAD

For this famous salad, created by the Tijuanan chef called Caesar Cardini in the 1920s, the dressing is traditionally tossed into crunchy Romaine lettuce, but any crisp lettuce will do.

INGREDIENTS

Serves 4
1 large Romaine lettuce
4 thick slices white or whole grain
  bread, crusts removed, cubed
3 tbsp olive oil
1 garlic clove, crushed

For the dressing
1 egg
1 garlic clove, chopped
2 tbsp lemon juice
dash of Worcestershire sauce
3 anchovy fillets, chopped
½ cup olive oil
5 tbsp grated Parmesan cheese
salt and black pepper

1 Preheat the oven to 425°F. Separate, rinse and dry the lettuce leaves. Tear the outer leaves roughly and chop the heart. Arrange the lettuce in a large salad bowl.

2 Mix together the cubed bread, olive oil and garlic in a separate bowl until the bread has soaked up the oil. Lay the bread cubes on a baking sheet and place in the oven for about 6–8 minutes (keeping an eye on them) until golden. Remove and leave to cool.

3 To make the dressing, break the egg into the bowl of a food processor or blender and add the garlic, lemon juice, Worcestershire sauce and one of the anchovy fillets. Blend until smooth.

4 With the motor running, pour in the olive oil in a thin stream until the dressing has the consistency of light cream. Season with black pepper and a little salt if needed.

5 Pour the dressing over the salad leaves and toss well, then toss in the garlic croûtons, Parmesan cheese and the remaining anchovies and serve.

CHINESE VEGETABLE STIR-FRY

A typical stir-fried vegetable dish popular all over China. Chinese leaves are like a cross between a cabbage and a crunchy lettuce, with a delicious peppery flavour.

INGREDIENTS

Serves 4
3 tbsp sunflower oil
1 tbsp sesame oil
1 garlic clove, chopped
2 cups broccoli florets, cut into
  small pieces
1 cup sugar snap peas
1 whole bok choy (about 1lb) or
  Savoy cabbage, sliced
4 scallions, finely chopped
2 tbsp soy sauce
2 tbsp dry sherry
1 tbsp sesame seeds, lightly
  toasted

1 Heat the oils in a wok or large frying pan until really hot, add the garlic and stir-fry for 30 seconds.

2 Add the broccoli florets and stir-fry for 3 minutes. Add the sugar snap peas and cook for 2 minutes, then toss in the bok choy or cabbage and the scallions and continue to stir-fry for a further 2 minutes.

3 Pour on the soy sauce, sherry and 2–3 tbsp water and stir-fry for a further 4 minutes, or until the vegetables are just tender. Sprinkle with the lightly toasted sesame seeds and serve hot.

MEDITERREAN MIXED PEPPER SALAD

INGREDIENTS

Serves 4
2 red bell peppers, halved and seeded
2 yellow bell peppers, halved and seeded
⅔ cup olive oil
1 onion, thinly sliced
2 garlic cloves, crushed
squeeze of lemon juice
chopped fresh parsley, to garnish

1 Grill the pepper halves for about 5 minutes, until the skin has blistered and blackened. Pop them into a plastic bag, seal and leave for 5 minutes.

2 Meanwhile, heat 2 tbsp of the olive oil in a frying pan and add the onion. Fry for about 5–6 minutes, until softened and translucent. Remove from the heat and reserve.

3 Take the peppers out of the bag and peel off the skins. Discard the skins and slice each pepper half into fairly thin strips.

4 Place the peppers, cooked onion and any oil from the pan into a bowl. Add the crushed garlic and pour on the remaining olive oil, add a good squeeze of lemon juice and season. Mix well, cover and marinate for 2–3 hours, stirring the mixture once or twice.

5 Garnish the pepper salad with chopped fresh parsley and serve either as a tasty appetizer or as an accompaniment to cold meats.

GREEK SPINACH AND CHEESE PIES

Makes 4
1 tbsp olive oil
1 small onion, finely chopped
10oz fresh spinach, well washed and
*   stalks removed*
4 tbsp butter, melted
4 sheets of filo pastry (about 18 x 10in)
1 egg
good pinch of grated nutmeg
¾ cup crumbled Feta cheese
1 tbsp grated Parmesan cheese
salt and black pepper

1 Preheat the oven to 375°F. Heat the oil in a pan, add the onion and fry gently for 5–6 minutes, until softened.

2 Add the spinach leaves and cook, stirring, until the spinach has wilted and some of the liquid has evaporated. Leave to cool.

3 Brush four 4in diameter loose-based tartlet pans with a little of the melted butter. Take two sheets of the filo pastry and cut each into eight 4½in squares. Keep the remaining filo sheets covered.

4 Brush four squares at a time with melted butter. Line the first tartlet pan with one square, gently easing it into the base and up the sides. Leave the edges overhanging.

5 Lay the remaining three buttered squares on top of the first, turning them so the corners form a star shape. Repeat for the remaining tartlet pans.

6 Beat the egg with the nutmeg and seasoning, then stir in the cheeses and spinach. Divide the mixture between the pans and level smooth. Fold the overhanging pastry back over the filling.

7 Cut one of the remaining sheets of pastry into eight 4in rounds. Brush with butter and place two on top of each tartlet. Press around the edges to seal. Brush the remaining sheet of pastry with butter and cut into strips. Gently twist each strip and lay on top of the tartlets. Leave to stand for 5 minutes, then bake for about 30–35 minutes, until golden. Serve hot or cold.

ZUCCHINI AND TOMATO BAKE

A *tian* is a heavy earthenware dish that many French vegetable dishes are cooked in. This typical peasant recipe is just one example.

INGREDIENTS

Serves 4

3 tbsp olive oil
1 onion, chopped
1 garlic clove, crushed
3 strips lean bacon, chopped
4 zucchini, grated
2 tomatoes, skinned, seeded and chopped
1 cup cooked long grain rice
2 tsp chopped fresh thyme
1 tbsp chopped fresh parsley
4 tbsp grated Parmesan cheese
2 eggs, lightly beaten
1 tbsp ricotta cheese
salt and black pepper

1 Preheat the oven to 350°F. Grease a shallow ovenproof dish with a little of the olive oil.

2 Heat the remaining oil in a frying pan, add the onion and garlic and fry for 5 minutes until softened.

3 Add the bacon and fry for 2 minutes, then stir in the zucchini and fry for a further 8 minutes, stirring occasionally and letting some of the liquid evaporate. Remove from the heat.

4 Add the tomatoes, rice, herbs, 2 tbsp of the Parmesan cheese, the beaten eggs, the ricotta cheese and seasoning and mix well.

5 Spoon the zucchini mixture into the dish and sprinkle over the remaining 2 tbsp of Parmesan cheese. Bake for 45 minutes, until set and golden. Serve hot.

COOK'S TIP
For a dinner party, divide the mixture among lightly greased individual gratin dishes and bake for about 25 minutes until set and golden.

MEXICAN RE-FRIED BEANS

In Mexico beans are served at every meal. In this recipe for *frijoles refritos* the beans are cooked once and then re-fried for extra flavor.

INGREDIENTS

Serves 4
2 tbsp sunflower oil
1 onion, diced
1 garlic clove, crushed
2 x 14oz cans red kidney beans
1 fresh green chili, seeded and diced
salt and black pepper

For re-frying the beans
3 tbsp vegetable oil
1 small onion, diced
1 fresh green chili, seeded and diced
natural yogurt, chopped scallions and
*   chili powder, to garnish*

1 Heat the oil in a pan and add the onion and garlic. Fry for 5–6 minutes, until the onion has softened and lightly browned.

2 Stir in the beans with the liquid from the cans, add the chili and a good pinch of salt. Bring to a boil, then cover and simmer gently for 45 minutes. Mash roughly with a potato masher and stir until thickened to a porridge consistency. Leave to cool.

3 To re-fry the beans, heat about 3 tbsp of oil in a pan and add the onion and chili. Fry for 5 minutes, then stir in the beans, pressing them down with the back of a spoon as they fry and then stirring so they don't burn. Repeat for about 5 minutes, until heated through, then season lightly.

4 Serve the beans topped with a spoonful of yogurt and a sprinkling of scallions and chili powder.

COOK'S TIP
The beans are delicious with lamb or pork chops, roast red meats, spicy sausages, or as a toast topper with shredded lettuce and sour cream.

SPANISH GREEN BEANS WITH HAM

Judias verdes con jamón are green beans cooked with a Spanish raw-cured dried Serrano ham – use prosciutto or unsmoked bacon as alternatives.

INGREDIENTS

Serves 4
1lb green beans
3 tbsp olive oil
1 onion, thinly sliced
2 garlic cloves, finely chopped
3oz prosciutto or bacon, chopped
salt and black pepper

1 Cook the beans in boiling salted water for about 5–6 minutes, until just tender but still with a bit of bite.

2 Meanwhile, heat the oil in a pan, add the onion and fry for 5 minutes, until softened and translucent. Add the garlic and prosciutto or bacon and cook for a further minute or two.

3 Drain the beans add to the pan and cook, stirring occasionally, for 2–3 minutes. Season well and serve hot.

CANDIED SWEET POTATOES WITH BACON

This sweet potato dish is always served for Thanksgiving in the United States to celebrate the settlers' first harvest.

──── INGREDIENTS ────

Serves 4

2 large sweet potatoes (1lb each), washed
½ cup soft light brown sugar
2 tbsp lemon juice
3 tbsp butter
4 strips smoked lean bacon, cut into matchsticks
salt and black pepper
fresh flat leaf parsley sprig, to garnish

1 Preheat the oven to 375°F and lightly butter a shallow ovenproof dish. Cut the unpeeled sweet potatoes crosswise into four and place the pieces in a large pot of boiling water. Cover the pot and cook for about 25 minutes, until just tender.

2 Drain and, when cool enough to handle, peel and slice quite thickly. Arrange in a single layer, overlapping, in the prepared dish.

3 Sprinkle over the sugar and lemon juice and dot with butter. Top with the bacon and season well.

4 Bake uncovered for 35–40 minutes, basting once or twice, until the potatoes are tender.

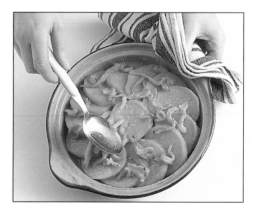

5 Preheat the broiler to a high heat. Broil the potatoes for 2–3 minutes, until they are browned and the bacon is crispy. Serve hot, garnished with parsley.

RATATOUILLE

Serves 4

2 large eggplants, roughly chopped
4 zucchini, roughly chopped
⅔ cup olive oil
2 onions, sliced
2 garlic cloves, chopped
1 large red bell pepper, seeded and
   roughly chopped
2 large yellow bell peppers, seeded and
   roughly chopped
fresh rosemary sprig
fresh thyme sprig
1 tsp coriander seeds, crushed
3 plum tomatoes, skinned, seeded
   and chopped
8 basil leaves, torn
salt and black pepper
fresh parsley or basil sprigs,
   to garnish

1 Sprinkle the eggplants and zucchini with salt, and then put them in a colander with a plate and weight on top to extract the bitter juices. Leave for about 30 minutes.

2 Heat the olive oil in a large saucepan. Add the onions, fry gently for about 6–7 minutes, until just softened, then add the garlic and cook for another 2 minutes.

3 Rinse the eggplants and zucchini and pat dry with paper towel. Add to the pan with the peppers, increase the heat and sauté until the peppers are just turning brown.

4 Add the herbs and coriander seeds, then cover the pan and cook gently for about 40 minutes.

5 Add the tomatoes and season well. Cook gently for a further 10 minutes, until the vegetables are soft but not too mushy. Remove the sprigs of herbs. Stir in the torn basil leaves and check the seasoning. Leave to cool slightly and serve warm or cold, garnished with sprigs of parsley or basil.

BOMBAY SPICED POTATOES

This Indian potato dish uses a mixture of whole and ground spices. Look out for mustard and black onion seeds in specialty food shops.

───── INGREDIENTS ─────

Serves 4

4 large potatoes, scrubbed, peeled and cubed
4 tbsp sunflower oil
1 garlic clove, finely chopped
2 tsp brown mustard seeds
1 tsp black onion seeds (optional)
1 tsp ground turmeric
1 tsp ground cumin
1 tsp ground coriander
1 tsp fennel seeds
salt and black pepper
good squeeze of lemon juice
chopped fresh coriander and lemon wedges, to garnish

1 Bring a pot of salted water to a boil, add the potatoes and simmer for about 4 minutes, until just tender. Drain thoroughly.

2 Heat the oil in a large frying pan and add the garlic along with all the whole and ground spices. Fry gently for 1–2 minutes, stirring until the mustard seeds start to pop.

3 Add the potatoes and stir-fry on a moderate heat for about 5 minutes, until heated through and well coated with the spicy oil.

4 Season well and sprinkle over the lemon juice. Garnish with chopped coriander and lemon wedges. Serve as an accompaniment to curries or other strong flavored meat dishes.

SPANISH CHILI POTATOES

The name of this Spanish *tapas* dish, *Patatas Bravas*, means fierce, hot potatoes. You can always reduce the amount of chili to suit your taste.

───── INGREDIENTS ─────

Serves 4

2lb new or salad potatoes
4 tbsp olive oil
1 onion, finely chopped
2 garlic cloves, crushed
1 tbsp tomato paste
7oz can chopped tomatoes
1 tbsp red wine vinegar
2–3 small dried red chilies, seeded and chopped finely, or 1–2 tsp hot chili powder
1 tsp paprika
salt and black pepper
1 fresh flat leaf parsley sprig, to garnish

1 Boil the potatoes in their skins for 10–12 minutes or until just tender. Drain well and leave to cool, then cut in half and reserve.

2 Heat the oil in a large pan and add the onion and garlic. Fry gently for 5–6 minutes, until just softened. Stir in the tomato paste, tomatoes, vinegar, chili and paprika, and then simmer for about 5 minutes.

3 Add the potatoes and mix into the sauce mixture until well coated. Cover and simmer gently for about 8–10 minutes, or until the potatoes are tender. Season well and transfer to a warmed serving dish. Serve garnished with a sprig of flat leaf parsley.

CHINESE CRISPY SEAWEED

In northern China they use a special kind of seaweed for this dish, but collards, shredded very finely, make a very good alternative. Serve either as an appetizer or as an accompaniment to a Chinese meal.

———— INGREDIENTS ————

Serves 4
8oz collards
groundnut or corn oil, for deep-frying
¼ tsp salt
2 tsp soft light brown sugar
2–3 tbsp flaked almonds, toasted

1 Cut out and discard any tough stalks from the collards. Place about six leaves on top of each other and roll up into a tight roll.

2 Using a sharp knife, slice across into thin shreds. Lay on a tray and leave to dry for about 2 hours.

3 Heat about 2–3in of oil in a wok or large heavy pan to 375°F. Carefully place a handful of the leaves into the oil – it will bubble and spit for the first 10 seconds and then die down. Deep-fry for about 45 seconds, or until a slightly darker green – be careful not to let the leaves burn.

4 Remove with a slotted spoon, drain on paper towel and transfer to a serving dish. Keep warm in the oven while frying the remainder.

5 When you have fried all the shredded leaves, sprinkle with the salt and sugar and toss lightly. Garnish with the toasted almonds.

> COOK'S TIP
> Make sure that your deep-frying pan is deep enough to allow the oil to bubble up during cooking. The pan should be less than half full.

LEEK AND PARSNIP PURÉE

Vegetable purées are popular in Britain and France served with meat, chicken or fish dishes. This mixture of leeks and parsnips makes a tasty accompaniment.

———— INGREDIENTS ————

Serves 4
2 large leeks, sliced
3 medium parsnips, sliced
½ tbsp butter
3 tbsp light cream
2 tbsp sour cream
good squeeze of lemon juice
salt and black pepper
good pinch of grated nutmeg,
  to garnish

1 Steam or boil the leeks and parsnips together for about 15 minutes, until tender. Drain well, then place in a food processor or blender.

2 Add the remaining ingredients to the processor or blender. Whizz until really smooth, then check the seasoning. Transfer to a warmed bowl and garnish with a sprinkling of nutmeg.

HOT DESSERTS

Hot, fragrant and delicious, here are desserts to warm up those chilly winter months or just to add the perfect finale to any meal. Favorite American classics are the Spiced Pumpkin Pie, and Creole Bread and Butter Pudding served with an irresistible hot whisky cream sauce. British favorites include Lemon Meringue Pie, and an Apple and Blackberry Nut Crumble that all purple-fingered blackberry-pickers would be proud of. From France come a bubbling pan of Crêpes Suzette, and a classic caramelized Upside-down Apple Tart – both dinner-party winners. Thai Fried Bananas make a delicious last-minute sweet and, if it's childhood classics you crave, try the steamed Austrian Nut Pudding with lashings of raspberry sauce.

AMERICAN SPICED PUMPKIN PIE

INGREDIENTS

Serves 4-6

1½ cups flour
pinch of salt
6 tbsp unsalted butter
1 tbsp superfine sugar
4 cups peeled fresh pumpkin, seeded
    and cubed, or 2 cups canned
    pumpkin, drained
⅝ cup soft light brown sugar
¼ tsp salt
¼ tsp ground allspice
½ tsp ground cinnamon
½ tsp ground ginger
2 eggs, lightly beaten
½ cup heavy cream
whipped cream, to serve

1 Place the flour in a bowl with the salt and butter and rub in with your fingertips until the mixture resembles bread crumbs (or use a food processor).

2 Stir in the sugar, add about 2–3 tbsp water and then mix to a soft dough. Knead the dough lightly on a floured surface. Flatten out into a round, wrap in a plastic bag and leave to chill for about 1 hour.

3 Preheat the oven to 400°F with a baking sheet inside. If you are using raw pumpkin for the pie, steam it for about 15 minutes, or until quite tender, then leave to cool completely. Purée the steamed or canned pumpkin in a food processor or blender until the consistency is very smooth.

4 Roll out the pastry quite thinly and use to line a 9½in (measured across the top) x 1in deep pie pan. Trim off any excess pastry and reserve for the decoration. Prick the base of the pie shell with a fork.

5 Cut as many leaf shapes as you can from the excess pastry and make vein markings with the back of a knife on each. Brush the edge of the pastry with water and stick the leaves all round the edge. Chill.

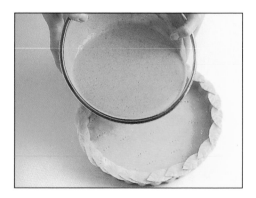

6 In a bowl mix together the pumpkin purée, sugar, salt, spices, eggs and cream and pour into the pie shell.

7 Place on the preheated baking sheet and bake for 15 minutes. Then reduce the temperature to 350°F and cook for a further 30 minutes, or until the filling is set and the crust is golden. Serve the pie warm with cream.

LEMON MERINGUE PIE

—— INGREDIENTS ——

Makes a 7½in pie
1 cup flour
4 tbsp butter, cubed
3 tbsp ground almonds
2 tbsp sugar
1 egg yolk

For the filling
juice of 3 lemons
finely grated rind of 2 lemons
3 tbsp cornstarch
6 tbsp sugar
2 egg yolks
1 tbsp butter

For the meringue
2 egg whites
⅝ cup superfine sugar

1 To make the pastry, sift the flour into a bowl, add the butter and rub in with your fingertips until the mixture resembles bread crumbs (or use a food processor). Stir in the almonds and sugar, and add the egg yolk and 2 tbsp cold water. Mix with your hands until the pastry comes together.

2 Knead the pastry lightly on a floured surface then wrap and chill for about 30 minutes. Meanwhile, pre-heat the oven to 400°F and put in a baking sheet to heat up.

3 Roll out the pastry to an 8in round and use it to line a 7½in fluted loose-based pie pan. Prick the base with a fork. Line with waxed paper and fill with baking beans.

4 Place the pan on the preheated baking sheet and bake for 12 minutes. Remove the paper and beans and bake for a further 5 minutes. Remove from the oven and cool. Reduce the temperature to 300°F.

5 To make the filling, put the lemon juice and rind into a measuring jug (you should have roughly ⅔ cup). Blend the cornstarch with a little of the lemon juice, then gradually stir in the rest. Pour into a saucepan and add ⅔ cup water.

6 Bring slowly to a boil, stirring until smooth and thickened. Remove from the heat and beat in the sugar and egg yolks, then add the butter. Spoon into the pie shell.

7 To make the meringue, whisk the egg whites until stiff, then gradually whisk in the sugar a tablespoon at a time until thick and glossy. Pile meringue on top of the lemon filling, spreading and swirling it with the back of a spoon. Bake for 30–35 minutes, or until the meringue is golden and crisp.

ZABAGLIONE

A much-loved, elegant Italian dessert traditionally made with Marsala, an Italian fortified wine. Madeira is a good alternative.

─────── INGREDIENTS ───────

Serves 4
4 egg yolks
4 tbsp sugar
4 tbsp Marsala or Madeira wine
Amaretti cookies, to serve

1 Place the egg yolks and sugar in a large heatproof bowl and whisk with an electric whisk until the mixture is pale and thick.

2 Gradually add the Marsala or Madeira, whisking well after each addition (at this stage the mixture will be quite runny).

3 Now place the bowl over a pan of gently simmering water and continue to whisk for at least 5–7 minutes, until the mixture becomes thick and mousse-like; when the beaters are lifted they should leave a thick trail on the surface of the mixture. (If you don't beat the mixture for long enough, the zabaglione will be too runny and will probably separate.)

4 Pour into four warmed, stemmed glasses and serve immediately with the Amaretti cookies for dipping.

> COOK'S TIP
> If you don't have any Marsala or Madeira you could use a medium sherry or a dessert wine.

MIXED BERRY SOUFFLÉ OMELET

These light French omelets take only a few minutes to cook and are best eaten straight away.

─────── INGREDIENTS ───────

Makes 2 (serves 4)
4 eggs, separated
finely grated rind of 1 lemon
2 tbsp sugar
drop of vanilla extract
1 tbsp light cream
2 tbsp butter
4 tbsp mixed berry preserve, warmed
confectioners' sugar, for dusting
2 tbsp toasted flaked almonds and fresh mint sprigs, to decorate

1 Place the egg yolks in a bowl and add the lemon rind, sugar, vanilla extract and cream. Beat with an electric or balloon whisk until pale and slightly thickened, then set aside.

2 Whisk the egg whites in a separate bowl until they hold stiff peaks. Gently beat 2 tbsp of the whisked whites into the egg yolk mixture to loosen it, then fold in the remainder using a large metal spoon.

3 Melt half the butter in a 9in frying pan and pour on half the egg mixture. Cook on a gentle heat for about 4 minutes, or until just set and lightly golden underneath.

4 Pop the pan under the hot broiler, for about 30 seconds, keeping a close eye on it until just browned. Remove from the broiler, and spoon half the warmed preserve over the omelet. Fold the omelet in half and slide it on to a warmed plate.

5 Dust with a little confectioners' sugar, sprinkle with half the almonds and decorate with mint. Cut in half and share between two people. Use the remaining mixture to make a second omelet.

CRÊPES SUZETTE

Makes 8
1 cup flour
pinch of salt
1 egg
1 egg yolk
1¼ cups low-fat (2% or 1%) milk
1 tbsp unsalted butter, melted, plus
extra for frying

For the sauce
2 large oranges
4 tbsp butter
½ cup soft light brown sugar
1 tbsp Grand Marnier
1 tbsp brandy

1 Sift the flour and salt into a bowl and make a well in the center. Crack the egg and extra yolk into the well.

2 Stir the eggs with a wooden spoon to incorporate the flour from around the edges. When the mixture thickens, gradually pour on the milk, beating well after each addition, until a smooth batter is formed.

3 Stir in the butter, transfer to a measuring jug, cover and chill.

4 Heat a medium (about 8in) shallow frying pan, add a little butter and heat until sizzling. Pour on a little of the batter, tilting the pan back and forth to cover the base thinly.

5 Cook over a medium heat for 1–2 minutes until lightly browned underneath, then flip over using a spatula and cook for a further minute. Repeat this process until you have eight crêpes. Stack them up on a plate, as they are ready.

6 Using a zester, pare the rind from one of the oranges and reserve about a teaspoon for decoration. Squeeze the juice from both oranges and set aside.

7 To make the sauce, melt the butter in a large frying pan and add the sugar with the orange rind and juice. Heat gently until the sugar has dissolved and the mixture is gently bubbling. Fold each crêpe in quarters. Add to the pan one at a time, coating them in the sauce and folding each one in half again. Gently move to the side of the pan to make room for the others.

8 Pour on the Grand Marnier and brandy and cook gently for 2–3 minutes, until the sauce has slightly caramelized. (For that extra touch, flame the brandy as you pour it into the pan.) Sprinkle with the reserved orange rind and serve straight from the pan.

CREOLE BREAD AND BUTTER PUDDING

────── INGREDIENTS ──────

Serves 4-6
4 ready-to-eat dried apricots, chopped
1 tbsp raisins
2 tbsp sultanas
1 tbsp chopped mixed citrus peel
1 loaf French bread (about 7oz),
  thinly sliced
4 tbsp butter, melted
1⅞ cups milk
⅔ cup heavy cream
⅝ cup sugar
3 eggs
½ tsp vanilla extract
2 tbsp whisky

For the cream
⅔ cup heavy cream
2 tbsp thick yogurt
1–2 tbsp whisky
1 tbsp sugar

1 Preheat the oven to 350°F. Lightly grease a deep 6 cup ovenproof baking dish with butter. Mix together the dried fruits and sprinkle a little over the base of the dish. Brush both sides of the bread slices with melted butter.

2 Fill the dish with alternate layers of bread slices and dried fruit, finishing with a layer of bread.

3 Heat the milk and cream together in a pan until just boiling. Meanwhile, place the sugar, eggs and vanilla extract in a bowl and whisk together.

4 Whisk the hot milk and cream into the eggs and then strain over the bread and fruit. Sprinkle the whisky over the top. Press the bread into the milk and egg mixture, cover with foil and leave to stand for 20 minutes.

5 Place the dish in a roasting pan half filled with water and bake for about 1 hour or until the custard is just set. Remove the foil and return the pudding to the oven to cook for a further 10 minutes, until the bread is golden.

6 Just before serving, place the cream, yogurt, whisky and sugar into a small pan, stir and heat gently. Serve with the hot pudding.

ORANGE RICE PUDDING

In Spain, Greece, Italy and Morocco rice puddings are a favorite dish, especially when sweetened with honey and flavored with orange.

INGREDIENTS

Serves 4
4 tbsp short grain rice
2½ cups milk
2–3 tbsp honey (according to taste)
finely grated rind of ½ small orange
⅔ cup heavy cream
1 tbsp chopped pistachio nuts,
  lightly toasted

1 Mix the rice with the milk, honey and orange rind in a saucepan and bring to a boil, then reduce the heat, cover and simmer very gently for about 1¼ hours, stirring regularly.

3 Pour in the cream and simmer for 5–8 minutes longer. Serve the rice sprinkled with the pistachio nuts in individual warmed bowls.

2 Remove the lid and cook, stirring for about 15–20 minutes, until the rice is tender and creamy.

APPLE AND BLACKBERRY NUT CRUMBLE

This much-loved dish of Bramley apples and blackberries topped with a golden, sweet crumble is perhaps one of the simplest and most delicious of British hot desserts.

INGREDIENTS

Serves 4
2lb (4 medium) cooking apples, peeled,
  cored and sliced
½ cup butter, cubed
⅝ cup soft light brown sugar,
  firmly packed
1¾ cups blackberries
¾ cup whole wheat flour
¾ cup flour
½ tsp ground cinnamon
3 tbsp chopped mixed nuts,
  toasted
custard, cream or ice cream, to serve

1 Preheat the oven to 350°F. Lightly butter a 5 cup ovenproof dish.

2 Place the apples in a pan with 2 tbsp of the butter, 2 tbsp of the sugar and 1 tbsp water. Cover and cook gently for about 10 minutes, until the apples are just tender but still holding their shape.

3 Remove from the heat and gently stir in the blackberries. Spoon the mixture into the ovenproof dish and set aside while you make the topping.

4 To make the crumble topping, sift the flours and cinnamon into a bowl (tip in any of the bran left in the sieve). Add the remaining 6 tbsp butter and rub into the flour with your fingertips until the mixture resembles fine bread crumbs (or you can use a food processor if you wish).

5 Stir in the remaining 6 tbsp sugar and the nuts and mix well. Sprinkle the crumble topping over the fruit. Bake for 35–40 minutes, until the top is golden brown. Serve hot with custard, cream or ice cream.

AUSTRIAN NUT PUDDING

INGREDIENTS

Serves 4

*4 tbsp superfine sugar, plus
 a little extra for sprinkling
1 cup chopped hazelnuts
4 tbsp butter, softened
2 eggs, separated
½ cup very fine fresh white
 bread crumbs
1¼ cups fresh raspberries
confectioners' sugar, to taste
whipped cream, to serve*

1 Preheat the oven to 325°F. Lightly grease a 1 quart ovenproof bowl and sprinkle evenly with a little superfine sugar.

2 Spread the hazelnuts on to a baking sheet and bake for 15–20 minutes, until toasted and golden. Remove from the oven and leave to cool.

3 Meanwhile, place the butter and sugar in a bowl and beat until pale and creamy. Beat in the egg yolks.

4 Process the cooled nuts in a food processor until finely ground.

5 Mix 1 tbsp water into the bread crumbs and beat into the creamed mixture with the hazelnuts.

6 Place the egg whites in a clean bowl and whisk until stiff. Beat about 2 tbsp into the creamed mixture to loosen it slightly and carefully fold in the remainder with a metal spoon.

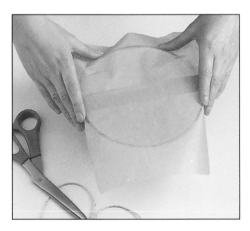

7 Spoon into the prepared basin and top with a circle of waxed paper with a fold in it, secured tightly with string. Cover with foil and steam for 1½ hours, checking and topping up the water level if it needs it.

8 Meanwhile, press the raspberries through a sieve into a bowl and add confectioners' sugar to sweeten according to taste. When the pudding is cooked, turn out and serve hot with the raspberry sauce and cream.

UPSIDE-DOWN APPLE TART

This delicious caramelized fruit tart from France, known as *Tarte Tatin,* was originally created by the Tatin sisters who ran a popular restaurant in Sologne in the Orléanais.

─────── INGREDIENTS ───────

Serves 4
For the pastry
4 tbsp butter, softened
3 tbsp superfine sugar
1 egg
1 cup flour
pinch of salt

For the apple layer
6 tbsp butter, softened
½ cup soft light brown sugar,
*   firmly packed*
10 firm, tart apples, peeled, cored and
*   thickly sliced*
whipped cream, to serve

1 To make the pastry, cream the butter and sugar in a bowl until pale and creamy. Beat in the egg, then sift in the flour and salt and mix to a soft dough. Knead lightly on a floured surface, then wrap and chill for 1 hour.

2 Grease a 9in cake pan, then add 4 tbsp of the butter. Place the cake pan on the burner and melt the butter gently. Remove and sprinkle over ⅓ cup of the sugar.

3 Arrange the apple slices on top, then sprinkle with the remaining sugar and dot with the remaining butter.

4 Preheat the oven to 450°F. Place the cake pan on the burner again over a low to medium heat for about 15 minutes, until a light golden caramel forms on the bottom. Remove the pan from the heat.

5 Roll out the pastry on a lightly floured surface to a round the same size as the pan and lay on top of the apples. Tuck the pastry edges down round the sides of the apples.

6 Bake for about 20–25 minutes, until the pastry is golden. Remove the tart from the oven and leave to stand for about 5 minutes.

7 Place an upturned plate on top of the pan and, holding the two together with a dish towel, turn the apple tart out on to the plate. Serve while still warm with whipped cream.

COOK'S TIP
It is important to use firm apples for this tart so that they will hold their shape well during cooking. Any type of firm eating apples will be suitable.

SPICED MEXICAN FRITTERS

Hot, sweet and spicy fritters are popular in both Spain and Mexico either for breakfast or as a mid-morning snack.

INGREDIENTS

Makes 16 (serves 4)
1¼ cups raspberries
3 tbsp confectioners' sugar
3 tbsp orange juice

For the fritters
4 tbsp butter
⅔ cup flour, sifted
2 eggs, lightly beaten
1 tbsp ground almonds
corn oil, for frying
1 tbsp confectioners' sugar and ½ tsp
  ground cinnamon, for dusting
8 fresh raspberries, to decorate

1 First make the raspberry sauce. Mash the raspberries with the confectioners' sugar and then push through a sieve into a bowl to remove all the seeds. Stir in the orange juice and chill while making the fritters.

2 To make the fritters, place the butter and ⅔ cup water in a saucepan and heat gently until the butter has melted. Bring to a boil and, when boiling, add the sifted flour all at once and turn off the heat.

3 Beat until the mixture leaves the sides of the pan and forms a ball. Cool slightly and beat in the eggs a little at a time, then add the almonds.

4 Spoon the mixture into a piping bag fitted with a large star nozzle. Half-fill a saucepan or deep-fat fryer with the oil and heat to 375°F.

5 Pipe about four 2in lengths at a time into the hot oil, cutting off the raw mixture with a knife as you go. Deep-fry for about 3–4 minutes, turning occasionally, until puffed up and golden. Drain on paper towel and keep warm in the oven while frying the remainder.

6 When you have fried all the mixture, dust the hot fritters with confectioners' sugar and cinnamon. Serve three or four per person on serving plates drizzled with a little of the raspberry sauce, dust again with sieved sugar and decorate with fresh raspberries.

THAI FRIED BANANAS

A very simple and quick Thai dessert – bananas fried in butter, brown sugar and lime juice, and then sprinkled with toasted coconut.

INGREDIENTS

Serves 4
3 tbsp butter
4 large slightly underripe bananas
1 tbsp shredded coconut
4 tbsp soft light brown sugar
4 tbsp lime juice
2 fresh lime slices, to decorate
thick and creamy natural yogurt,
  to serve

1 Heat the butter in a large frying pan or wok and fry the bananas for 1–2 minutes on each side, or until they are lightly golden in color.

2 Meanwhile, dry-fry the coconut in a small frying pan until lightly browned and reserve.

3 Sprinkle the sugar into the pan with the bananas, add the lime juice and cook, stirring until dissolved. Sprinkle the coconut over the bananas, decorate with lime slices and serve with the thick and creamy yogurt.

APPLE STRUDEL

This Austrian dessert is traditionally made with paper-thin layers of buttered strudel pastry, filled with spiced apples and nuts. Ready-made filo pastry makes an easy substitute.

INGREDIENTS

Serves 4-6
¾ chopped hazelnuts, roasted
2 tbsp almonds, roasted
4 tbsp raw sugar
½ tsp ground cinnamon
grated rind and juice of ½ lemon
2 large firm, tart cooking apples,
   peeled, cored and chopped
⅓ cup sultanas
4 large sheets filo pastry
4 tbsp unsalted butter, melted
confectioners' sugar, for dusting
cream, custard or yogurt, to serve

1 Preheat the oven to 375°F. In a bowl mix together the hazelnuts, almonds, sugar, ground cinnamon, lemon rind and juice, apples and sultanas, then set aside.

2 Lay one sheet of filo pastry on a clean dish towel and brush with melted butter. Lay a second sheet on top and brush again with melted butter. Repeat with the remaining two sheets.

3 Spread the fruit and nut mixture over the pastry, leaving a 3in border at each of the shorter ends. Fold the pastry ends in over the filling. Roll up from one long edge to the other, using the dish towel to help.

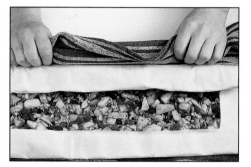

4 Carefully transfer the strudel to a greased baking sheet, placing the seam side down. Brush all over with butter and bake for 30–35 minutes, until golden and crisp. Dust with confectioners' sugar and serve while still hot with cream, custard or yogurt.

CHOCOLATE FRUIT FONDUE

Fondues originated in Switzerland, and this sweet treat is the perfect ending to any meal.

INGREDIENTS

Serves 6-8
16 fresh strawberries
4 rings fresh pineapple, cut into wedges
2 small nectarines, pitted and cut
   into wedges
1 kiwi fruit, halved and thickly sliced
small bunch of black seedless grapes
2 bananas, chopped
1 small eating apple, cored and cut
   into wedges
lemon juice, for brushing
8oz semisweet chocolate
1 tbsp butter
⅔ cup light cream
3 tbsp Irish cream liqueur
1 tbsp pistachio nuts, chopped

1 Arrange the fruit on a serving platter and brush the banana and apple pieces with a little lemon juice. Cover and chill until ready to serve.

2 Place the chocolate, butter, cream and liqueur in a heatproof bowl over a pan of gently simmering water. Stir occasionally until melted and completely smooth.

3 Pour the chocolate mixture into a warmed serving bowl and sprinkle with the pistachios. To serve, guests help themselves by skewering fruits on to fondue forks or dessert forks and dipping in the hot chocolate sauce.

COLD DESSERTS

Perhaps the best thing about cold desserts is that you can make them well in advance and avoid all those last-minute panics! Another wonderful thing is that they taste so good. In this chapter are a selection of international classics, some with new twists but all guaranteed to be easy to make. For instant success, try Chinese Fruit Salad steeped in a lime syrup, a British Rhubarb and Orange Fool, Italian Apricots with Orange Cream, or the Greek Fig and Honey Dessert. For special occasions, the American classic Mississippi Pecan Pie, and Crème Caramel from France are all-time favorites, and the Australian Hazelnut Pavlova is bound to impress the guests. For ice cream fanatics, Rippled Chocolate Ice Cream is unbeatable, but for a change try the flavor of the Far East in the delicious Mango Ice Cream, packed with fruit.

CRÈME CARAMEL

The classic, creamy, caramel-flavored custard from France.

---INGREDIENTS---

Serves 4-6
½ *cup granulated sugar*
1¼ *cups milk*
1¼ *cups light cream*
6 *eggs*
6 *tbsp superfine sugar*
½ *tsp vanilla extract*

1 Preheat the oven to 300°F and half-fill a large, deep roasting pan with water.

2 Place the granulated sugar in a small saucepan with 4 tbsp water and heat it gently, swirling the pan from time to time, until the sugar has dissolved. Increase the heat and boil to a good caramel color.

3 Immediately pour the caramel into an ovenproof soufflé dish. Place in the roasting pan and set aside.

4 To make the egg custard, heat the milk and cream together in a pan until almost boiling. Meanwhile, beat the eggs, superfine sugar and vanilla extract together in a bowl using a large balloon whisk.

5 Whisk the hot milk into the eggs and sugar, then strain the liquid through a sieve into the soufflé dish, on top of the cooled caramel base.

6 Transfer the pan to the oven and bake in the center for about 1½–2 hours (topping up the water level after 1 hour), or until the custard has set in the center. Lift the dish carefully out of the water and leave to cool, then cover and chill overnight.

7 Loosen the sides of the chilled custard with a knife and then place an inverted plate (large enough to hold the caramel sauce that will flow out as well) on top of the dish. Holding the dish and plate together, turn upside down and give a quick shake to release the crème caramel.

AUSTRALIAN HAZELNUT PAVLOVA

INGREDIENTS

Serves 4-6
3 egg whites
⅞ cup superfine sugar
1 tsp cornstarch
1 tsp white wine vinegar
5 tbsp chopped hazelnuts,
   roasted
1 cup heavy cream
1 tbsp orange juice
2 tbsp thick and creamy natural yogurt
2 ripe nectarines, pitted and sliced
2 cups raspberries, halved
1–2 tbsp red currant or raspberry
   jelly, warmed

1 Preheat the oven to 275°F. Lightly grease a baking sheet. Draw an 8in circle on a sheet of parchment paper. Place pencil-side down on the greased baking sheet.

2 Place the egg whites in a clean, grease-free bowl and whisk with an electric mixer until stiff. Whisk in the sugar 1 tbsp at a time, whisking well after each addition.

3 Add the cornstarch, vinegar and hazelnuts and fold in carefully with a large metal spoon.

4 Spoon the meringue on to the marked circle and spread out to the edges, making a dip in the center.

5 Bake for about 1¼–1½ hours, until crisp. Leave to cool completely and transfer to a serving platter.

6 Whip the cream and orange juice until just thick, stir in the yogurt and spoon on to the meringue. Top with the fruit and drizzle over the warmed jelly. Serve immediately.

CHINESE FRUIT SALAD

For an unusual fruit salad with an oriental flavor, try this mixture of fruits in a tangy lime and lychee syrup topped with a light sprinkling of toasted sesame seeds.

―――――INGREDIENTS―――――

Serves 4
½ cup superfine sugar
thinly pared rind and juice of 1 lime
14oz can lychees in syrup
1 ripe mango, pitted and sliced
1 eating apple, cored and sliced
2 bananas, chopped
1 star fruit, sliced (optional)
1 tsp sesame seeds, toasted

1 Place the sugar in a saucepan with 1¼ cups water and the pared lime rind. Heat gently until the sugar dissolves, then increase the heat and boil gently for about 7–8 minutes. Remove the pan from the heat and leave on one side to cool.

2 Drain the lychees into a measuring jug and pour the juice into the cooled lime syrup with the lime juice. Place all the prepared fruit in a bowl and pour over the lime and lychee syrup. Chill for 1 hour. Sprinkle with toasted sesame seeds to serve.

APRICOT AND ALMOND JALOUSIE

Jalousie means "shutter" in French, and the traditional slatted puff pastry topping of this fruit pie looks exactly like the shutters which adorn the windows of French houses.

―――――INGREDIENTS―――――

Serves 4
8oz ready-made puff pastry
a little beaten egg
6 tbsp apricot preserve
2 tbsp sugar
2 tbsp flaked almonds
cream or natural yogurt, to serve

1 Preheat the oven to 425°F. Roll out the pastry on a lightly floured surface and cut into a 12in square. Cut in half to make two rectangles.

2 Place one piece of pastry on a wetted baking sheet and brush all round the edges with beaten egg. Spread over the apricot preserve.

3 Fold the remaining rectangle in half lengthwise and cut about eight diagonal slits from the center fold to within about ½in from the edge all the way along.

4 Unfold the pastry and lay it on top of the preserve-covered pastry on the baking sheet. Press the pastry edges together well to seal and knock up with the back of a knife.

5 Brush the slashed pastry with water and sprinkle over the sugar and the flaked almonds.

6 Bake in the oven for 25–30 minutes, until well risen and golden brown. Remove the jalousie from the oven and leave to cool. Serve sliced, with cream or natural yogurt.

COOK'S TIP
Use other flavors of fruit preserve to fill the jalousie, or, if you prefer, substitute some canned fruit pie filling instead. You could also make smaller, individual jalousies to serve with morning coffee, if you like.

Baked American Cheesecake

Makes 9 squares
For the base
1½ cups crushed graham crackers
3 tbsp butter, melted

For the topping
2½ cups farmers' cheese or
  cream cheese
½ cup superfine sugar
3 eggs
finely grated rind of 1 lemon
1 tbsp lemon juice
½ tsp vanilla extract
1 tbsp cornstarch
2 tbsp sour cream
⅔ cup sour cream and ¼ tsp ground
  cinnamon, to decorate

1 Preheat the oven to 325°F. Lightly grease and line a 7in square loose-based pan.

2 Place the crushed crackers and butter in a bowl and mix well. Tip into the base of the prepared cake pan and press down firmly with a potato masher.

3 Place the cheese in a bowl, add the sugar and beat well until smooth. Add the eggs one at a time, beating well after each addition and then stir in the lemon rind and juice, the vanilla extract, cornstarch and sour cream. Beat until smooth.

4 Pour the mixture on to the cracker base and level out. Bake for 1¼ hours, or until the cheesecake has set in the center. Turn off the oven and leave inside until completely cold.

5 Remove the cheesecake from the pan, top with the sour cream and swirl with the back of a spoon. Sprinkle with cinnamon and cut into squares.

MANGO ICE CREAM

Mangoes are used widely in Far Eastern cooking, particularly in Thailand, where they are used to make this deliciously rich and creamy ice cream.

─────── INGREDIENTS ───────

Serves 4-6

2 x 15oz cans sliced mango,
 drained
4 tbsp sugar
2 tbsp lime juice
1 tbsp powdered gelatin
1½ cups heavy cream, lightly whipped
fresh mint sprigs, to decorate

1 Reserve four slices of mango for decoration and chop the remainder. Place the mangoes in a bowl with the sugar and lime juice.

2 Put 3 tbsp hot water in a small bowl and sprinkle over the gelatin. Place over a pot of gently simmering water and stir until dissolved. Pour on to the mangoes and mix well.

3 Add the lightly whipped cream and fold into the mango mixture. Pour the mixture into a plastic freezer container and freeze for 2–3 hours.

4 Place in a food processor or blender and blend until smooth. Spoon back into the plastic container and re-freeze.

5 Remove from the freezer 10 minutes before serving and place in the fridge. Serve scoops of ice cream decorated with pieces of the reserved sliced mango and fresh mint sprigs.

GREEK FIG AND HONEY DESSERT

A quick and easy dessert made from fresh or canned figs topped with thick and creamy yogurt, drizzled with honey and sprinkled with pistachio nuts.

INGREDIENTS

Serves 4

4 *fresh or canned figs*
2 x 8oz *tubs/2 cups thick and creamy*
  natural yogurt
4 tbsp *honey*
2 tbsp *chopped pistachio nuts*

1 Chop the figs and place in the bottom of four stemmed glasses or deep, individual dessert bowls.

2 Top each glass or bowl of figs with ½ cup of the thick yogurt. Chill until ready to serve.

3 Just before serving drizzle 1 tbsp honey over each dessert and sprinkle with the pistachio nuts.

COOK'S TIP
Look out for exotic honeys made from the nectar of flowers like lavender, clover, acacia, heather, rosemary and thyme.

RUSSIAN FRUIT COMPÔTE

This fruit pudding is traditionally called *Kissel* and is made from the thickened juice of stewed red or black currants. This recipe uses the whole fruit with added blackberry liqueur.

INGREDIENTS

Serves 4

2 cups *red or black currants, or*
  a mixture of both
2 cups *raspberries*
⅔ cup *water*
4 tbsp *superfine sugar*
1½ tbsp *arrowroot*
1–2 tbsp *blackberry liqueur*
natural yogurt, to serve

1 Place the red or black currants and raspberries, water and sugar in a pan. Cover the pan and cook gently over a low heat for 12–15 minutes, until the fruit is soft.

2 Blend the arrowroot with a little water in a small bowl and stir into the hot fruit mixture. Bring the fruit mixture back to a boil, stirring all the time, until thickened and smooth.

3 Remove the pan from the heat and leave the fruit compôte to cool slightly, and then gently stir in the blackberry liqueur.

4 Pour the compôte into four glass serving bowls and leave until cold, then chill until required. Serve topped with spoonfuls of yogurt.

COOK'S TIP
Instead of blackberry liqueur you could use Crème de Cassis, raspberry liqueur, plum brandy or Kirsch, if you prefer.

MISSISSIPPI PECAN PIE

Makes an 8in pie
For the pastry
1 cup flour
4 tbsp butter, cubed
2 tbsp sugar
1 egg yolk

For the filling
5 tbsp corn syrup
⅓ cup dark brown sugar, firmly packed
4 tbsp butter
3 eggs, lightly beaten
½ tsp vanilla extract
1¼ cups pecan nuts
fresh cream or ice cream, to serve

1 Place the flour in a bowl and add the butter. Rub in with your fingertips until the mixture resembles bread crumbs, then stir in the sugar, egg yolk and about 2 tbsp cold water. Mix to a dough and knead lightly on a floured surface until smooth.

2 Roll out the pastry on a floured surface and use to line an 8in loose-based fluted pie pan. Prick the base, then line with waxed paper and fill with baking beans. Chill for 30 minutes. Preheat the oven to 400°F.

3 Bake the pie shell for 10 minutes. Remove the paper and beans and bake for 5 minutes. Reduce the oven temperature to 350°F.

4 Meanwhile, heat the syrup, sugar and butter in a pan until the sugar dissolves. Remove from the heat and cool slightly. Whisk in the eggs and vanilla extract and stir in the pecans.

5 Pour into the pie shell and bake for 35–40 minutes, until the filling is set. Serve with cream or ice cream.

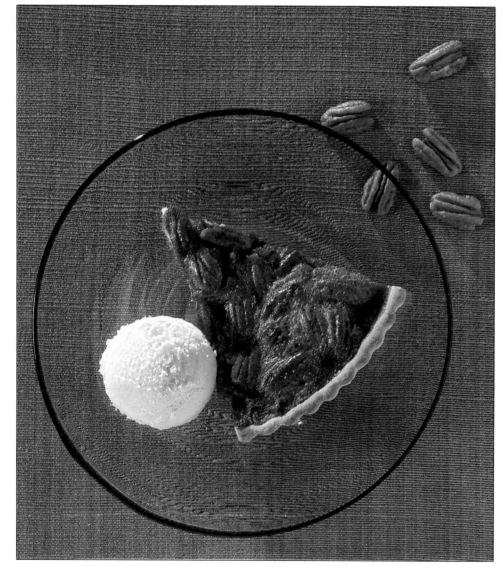

BOSTON BANOFFEE PIE

Makes an 8in pie
1¼ cups flour
1 cup butter
4 tbsp superfine sugar
½ x 14oz can skimmed, sweetened
    condensed milk
⅔ cup soft light brown sugar
2 tbsp corn syrup
2 small bananas, sliced
a little lemon juice
whipped cream, to decorate
1 tsp grated semisweet chocolate

1 Preheat the oven to 325°F. Place the flour and ½ cup of the butter in a food processor and blend until crumbed (or rub in with your fingertips). Stir in the superfine sugar.

2 Squeeze the mixture together with your hands until it forms a dough. Press into the base of an 8in loose-based fluted pie pan. Bake for 25–30 minutes, until lightly browned.

3 Place the remaining ½ cup butter with the condensed milk, brown sugar and syrup into a large non-stick saucepan and heat gently, stirring all the time, until the butter has melted and the sugar has dissolved.

4 Bring to a gentle boil and cook for 7 minutes, stirring all the time to prevent burning, until the mixture thickens and turns a light caramel color. Pour on to the cooked pastry base and leave until cold.

5 Sprinkle the bananas with lemon juice and arrange in overlapping circles on top of the caramel filling, leaving a gap in the center. Pipe a swirl of whipped cream in the center and sprinkle with the grated chocolate.

APRICOTS WITH ORANGE CREAM

Mascarpone is a very rich cream cheese made from thick Lombardy cream. It is delicious flavored with orange as a topping for these poached, chilled apricots.

INGREDIENTS

Serves 4

2½ cups ready-to-eat dried apricots
strip of lemon peel
1 cinnamon stick
2 tbsp sugar
⅔ cup sweet dessert wine (such as Muscat de Beaumes de Venise or Sauternes)
½ cup Mascarpone cream cheese or sour cream
3 tbsp orange juice
2 tsp sugar
pinch of ground cinnamon and fresh mint sprig, to decorate

1 Place the dried apricots, lemon peel and cinnamon stick in a pan and cover with 1⅞ cups cold water. Bring to a boil, cover the pan and then simmer gently for about 25 minutes, until the fruit is tender.

2 Remove from the heat and stir in the dessert wine. Leave until cold, then chill for 3–4 hours or overnight.

3 Mix together the Mascarpone cheese or sour cream, orange juice and sugar in a bowl and beat well until smooth. Chill until required.

4 Just before serving remove the cinnamon stick and lemon peel from the apricots and serve with a spoonful of the chilled Mascarpone orange cream sprinkled with a little cinnamon and decorated with a sprig of fresh mint.

RHUBARB AND ORANGE FOOL

Perhaps this traditional English pudding got its name because it is so easy to make that even a "fool" can attempt it.

INGREDIENTS

Serves 4

2 tbsp orange juice
1 tsp finely pared orange rind
2lb (about 10–12 stems) rhubarb, peeled and chopped
1 tbsp red currant jelly
3 tbsp superfine sugar
⅔ cup heavy cream
5oz prepared thick and creamy vanilla custard
sweet cookies, to serve

1 Place the orange juice and rind, the rhubarb, red currant jelly and sugar into a saucepan. Cover and simmer gently for about 8 minutes, stirring occasionally, until the rhubarb is just tender but not mushy.

2 Remove the pan from the heat, transfer the rhubarb to a bowl and leave to cool completely. Meanwhile, beat the cream lightly.

3 Drain the cooled rhubarb to remove some of the liquid. Reserve about 2 tbsp of the rhubarb and a little orange rind for decoration. Purée the remaining rhubarb in a food processor or blender, or push through a sieve.

4 Stir the custard into the purée, then fold in the whipped cream. Spoon the fool into individual bowls, cover and chill. Just before serving, top with the reserved fruit and rind. Serve with crisp, sweet cookies.

RIPPLED CHOCOLATE ICE CREAM

Rich, smooth and packed with chocolate, this heavenly ice cream is an all-round-the-world chocaholics' favorite – and it's so easy to make.

──────── INGREDIENTS ────────

Serves 4

4 tbsp store-bought chocolate and
   hazelnut spread
1⅛ cups heavy cream
1 tbsp confectioners' sugar, sifted
5 tbsp chopped semisweet
   chocolate
chocolate curls, to decorate

1 Mix together the chocolate and hazelnut spread and 5 tbsp of the heavy cream in a bowl.

2 Place the remaining cream and the confectioners' sugar in a second bowl and beat until softly whipped.

3 Lightly fold in the chocolate mixture with the chopped chocolate until the mixture is rippled. Transfer to a plastic freezer container and freeze for about 3–4 hours, until firm.

4 Remove the ice cream from the freezer about 10 minutes before serving to allow it to soften slightly. Spoon or scoop into dessert dishes or glasses and top each serving with a few chocolate curls.

ORANGES WITH SAFFRON YOGURT

After a hot and spicy curry, a popular Indian dessert is simply sliced, juicy oranges sprinkled with a little cinnamon and served with a spoonful of saffron-flavored yogurt.

──────── INGREDIENTS ────────

Serves 4

4 large oranges
¼ tsp ground cinnamon
5oz natural yogurt
2 tsp sugar
3–4 saffron strands
¼ tsp ground ginger
1 tbsp chopped pistachio nuts,
   toasted
fresh lemon balm or mint leaves,
   to decorate

┌─────────────────────────────┐
│ COOK'S TIP
│ If you haven't any oranges to
│ hand, you could use clementines
│ or the deliciously juicy blood
│ oranges when they are in season.
└─────────────────────────────┘

1 Slice the bottoms off each of the oranges so they sit upright on a board. Working from the top of the orange, cut across the top and down one side. Follow the contours of the orange to reveal the orange flesh just beneath the pith. Repeat until all the peel and pith has been removed, reserving any juice. Peel the remaining oranges in the same way.

2 Slice the oranges thinly and remove any seeds. Lay in a single layer, overlapping the slices, on a shallow serving platter. Sprinkle over the ground cinnamon, then cover and chill.

3 Mix the yogurt, sugar, saffron and ginger together in a bowl and leave to stand for 5 minutes. Spoon into a serving bowl and sprinkle with the nuts. Spoon a little of the yogurt mixture on to each serving and decorate with lemon balm or mint.

CAKES AND COOKIES

They always say you leave the best till last, so – if you feel you deserve a sweet treat – then look no further. When people are asked about their worldwide favorites, American Chocolate Fudge Brownies and Blueberry Muffins are often top of the list, while cream-filled Chocolate Profiteroles from France come a close second. Other popular bakes include Sticky Gingerbread, a traditional British recipe that is absolutely delicious served still slightly warm. From Holland comes a wonderful deep apple tart with a melt-in-the-mouth pastry, and from Austria comes a delicious raspberry tart; both are hard to resist. If it's something more savory that you're after, you may find that the Italian Olive Bread will not be allowed to cool down before it is gobbled up.

CLARE'S AMERICAN CARROT CAKE

INGREDIENTS

Makes an 8in round cake

1 cup corn oil
1¼ cups granulated sugar
3 eggs
1½ cups flour
1½ tsp baking powder
1½ tsp baking soda
¾ tsp salt
1½ tsp ground cinnamon
good pinch of grated nutmeg
¼ tsp ground ginger
1 cup chopped walnuts
8oz (2 large) carrots, finely grated
1 tsp vanilla extract
2 tbsp sour cream

For the frosting

1 cup whole cream cheese
2 tbsp butter, softened
2 cups confectioners' sugar, sifted
*8 tiny carrots made from orange and
  green colored marzipan, to decorate*

1 Preheat the oven to 350°F. Grease two 8in loose-based round cake pans and line the bases with waxed or parchment paper.

2 Put the corn oil and sugar into a bowl and beat well. Add the eggs, one at a time, and beat them very thoroughly into the mixture.

3 Sift the flour, baking powder, baking soda, salt, cinnamon and nutmeg into the bowl and beat well. Fold in the chopped walnuts and grated carrots and stir in the vanilla extract and sour cream.

4 Divide the mixture between the prepared pans and bake in the center of the oven for about 1 hour 5 minutes, or until well risen and springy to touch in the center (a skewer pierced through the center should come out clean).

5 Leave to cool in the pans on a wire rack. Meanwhile, mix together all the ingredients for the frosting in a bowl. Beat until smooth.

6 Turn the cooled cakes out of the pans and sandwich them together with a little of the frosting. Spread the remaining frosting over the top of the cake and down the sides, making a swirling pattern with a round-bladed knife. Decorate with the marzipan carrots just before serving.

STICKY GINGERBREAD

INGREDIENTS

Makes a 2lb loaf
1½ cups flour
2 tsp ground ginger
½ tsp cinnamon
½ tsp baking soda
2 tbsp black molasses
2 tbsp corn syrup
⅝ cup soft dark brown sugar
6 tbsp butter
1 egg
1 tbsp milk
1 tbsp orange juice
2 pieces preserved ginger, finely chopped
½ cup sultanas
5 ready-to-eat dried apricots, chopped
3 tbsp confectioners' sugar
2 tsp lemon juice

1 Preheat the oven to 325°F. Grease and line the base a 2lb loaf pan with waxed paper. Sift the flour, spices and baking soda into a bowl.

2 Place the molasses, syrup, sugar and butter in a pan and heat gently until the butter has melted.

3 In a separate small bowl beat the egg, milk and orange juice together.

4 Add the syrup, egg mixture, chopped ginger, sultanas and apricots to the dry ingredients and stir well. Spoon into the prepared pan and level out. Bake in the oven for about 50 minutes, or until the gingerbread is well risen and a skewer pierced through the center comes out clean.

5 When cooked, remove from the oven, and leave to cool in the pan. Mix the confectioners' sugar with the lemon juice in a bowl and beat until smooth. Drizzle the icing back and forth over the top of the gingerbread, leave to set, then cut into thick slices to serve.

CHOCOLATE PROFITEROLES

These luscious French pastries are often served as a dessert.

INGREDIENTS

Makes 24
⅔ cup flour
pinch of salt
4 tbsp butter
2 eggs, beaten
1⅛ cups whipping cream
4oz semisweet chocolate

1 Preheat the oven to 425°F. Grease two baking sheets. Sift the flour and salt on to a sheet of paper. Put the butter and ⅔ cup water into a saucepan and heat gently until the butter has melted. Bring to a boil and then quickly tip in the flour all at once.

2 Remove from the heat. Beat until the mixture forms a ball and leaves the sides of the pan. Cool slightly.

3 Gradually add the beaten eggs, beating well after each addition, until a smooth, thick paste is formed. Spoon into a large piping bag fitted with a ½in plain nozzle.

4 Pipe 24 walnut-sized balls on to the baking sheets. Place on the top shelves of the oven and bake for 20–25 minutes, until well risen and golden. Remove and make a slit in each one to allow the steam to escape, then return to the oven for 5 minutes. Cool the profiteroles on a wire rack.

5 Place all but 4 tbsp of the cream in a bowl, whip until just thick and spoon into a large piping bag fitted with a plain nozzle. Cut each bun in half, fill with cream and reassemble.

6 To make the chocolate sauce, place the chocolate in a pan with 4 tbsp water and the reserved 4 tbsp cream. Heat gently over a very low heat until the chocolate has melted. Serve four to six profiteroles per person on small plates with the hot chocolate sauce poured over.

MEXICAN CINNAMON COOKIES

Shortbread cookies called *pastelitos* are traditionally served at Mexican weddings. These little sweet cookies are dusted with confectioners' sugar to match the bride's wedding dress.

INGREDIENTS

Makes 20
½ cup butter
2 tbsp sugar
1 cup flour
½ cup cornstarch
¼ tsp ground cinnamon
2 tbsp chopped mixed nuts
3 tbsp confectioners' sugar, sifted

1 Preheat the oven to 325°F. Lightly grease a baking tray. Place the butter and sugar in a bowl and beat until pale and creamy.

2 Sift in the plain flour, cornstarch and cinnamon and gradually work in with a wooden spoon until the mixture comes together. Knead lightly until completely smooth.

3 Take tablespoonfuls of the mixture, roll into 20 small balls and arrange on the baking tray. Press a few chopped nuts into the top of each one and then flatten slightly.

4 Bake the cookies for about 30–35 minutes, until pale golden. Remove from the oven and, while they are still warm, toss them in the sifted confectioners' sugar. Leave the cookies to cool on a wire rack before serving.

DUTCH APPLE TART

Makes an 8in round tart
1½ cups flour
9 tbsp butter, cubed and softened
6 tbsp superfine sugar
pinch of salt
6 medium eating apples, peeled, cored
and grated
4 tbsp soft light brown sugar
¼ tsp vanilla extract
½ tsp ground cinnamon
3 tbsp raisins
4 tbsp flaked almonds, toasted
1 tbsp superfine sugar, for sprinkling
whipped cream, to serve

1 Preheat the oven to 350°F. Lightly butter an 8in round springform pan and dust with a little plain flour.

2 Place the flour in a bowl with the butter and sugar, then squeeze together to form a firm dough. Knead lightly, then wrap and chill for 1 hour.

3 Roll two-thirds of the chilled pastry out on a lightly floured surface to form a 10in round and use to line the base and two-thirds up the sides of the pan, pressing the pastry up the sides with your fingers.

4 Mix together the apples, sugar, vanilla extract, cinnamon, raisins and almonds in a bowl. Spoon into the lined pan and level the surface. Fold the pastry edge above the level of the apples down over the filling.

5 Roll out the remaining pastry and cut into eight ½in strips. Brush the strips with cold water and sprinkle over the superfine sugar. Lay on top of the tart in a lattice, securing the ends to the folded-over edge with water.

6 Bake in the center of the oven for 1 hour, or until the pastry is golden. Remove and leave to cool in the pan. When the tart is cold, carefully remove from the pan. Cut into slices and serve with whipped cream.

BAKLAVA

This sweet and spicy pie from Greece and Turkey is made with layers of buttered filo pastry packed with nuts and sweetened with a honey and lemon syrup.

INGREDIENTS

Makes 10 pieces
6 tbsp butter, melted
6 large sheets of filo pastry
2 cups chopped mixed nuts (such as almonds, pistachios, hazelnuts and walnuts)
1 cup fresh bread crumbs
1 tsp ground cinnamon
1 tsp allspice
½ tsp grated nutmeg
1 cup honey
4 tbsp lemon juice

1 Preheat the oven to 350°F. Grease a 7 x 11in shallow baking pan. Unroll the pastry, brush one sheet with melted butter (keep the remainder covered with a dish towel while you work) and use to line the pan, easing it carefully up the sides.

2 Brush two more sheets with butter and lay on top of the base sheet, easing the pastry into the corners and letting the edges overhang.

3 Mix together the nuts, bread crumbs and spices in a bowl and spoon this mixture into the lined pan.

4 Cut the remaining three sheets of pastry in half widthwise and brush each one with a little of the butter. Layer the sheets on top of the filling and fold in any overhanging edges.

5 Top with the remaining buttered sheets. Cut the baklava diagonally into diamonds. Bake in the oven for about 30 minutes, until golden.

6 Meanwhile, heat the honey and lemon juice together in a saucepan. When the baklava is cooked, remove from the oven and pour over the syrup while still warm. Leave to cool completely, re-cut into diamonds and serve.

BLUEBERRY MUFFINS

Hot blueberry muffins with a hint of vanilla are an American favorite for breakfast, a mid-morning snack or tea. Make a batch with your children – you'll find that they will love to help cook – and eat – them.

INGREDIENTS

Makes 12
3 cups flour
2 tsp baking powder
¼ tsp salt
½ cup sugar
2 eggs, beaten
1¼ cups milk
½ cup butter, melted
1 tsp vanilla extract
1⅓ cups blueberries

1 Preheat the oven to 400°F. Grease a 12 hole muffin pan.

2 Sift the flour, baking powder and salt into a large mixing bowl and stir in the sugar.

3 Place the eggs, milk, butter and vanilla extract in a separate bowl and whisk together well.

4 Fold the egg mixture into the dry ingredients with a metal spoon, then gently stir in the blueberries.

5 Spoon the mixture into the muffin holes, filling them until just below the top. Place the muffin pan on the top shelf of the oven and bake for 20–25 minutes, until the muffins are well risen and lightly browned. Leave the muffins in the pan for 5 minutes and then turn them out on to a wire rack to cool. Serve warm or cold.

AMERICAN CHOCOLATE FUDGE BROWNIES

INGREDIENTS

Makes 12 pieces
¾ cup butter
6 tbsp cocoa powder
2 eggs, lightly beaten
1¼ cups soft light brown sugar
½ tsp vanilla extract
1 cup chopped pecan nuts
½ cup self-rising flour

For the frosting
4oz semisweet chocolate
2 tbsp butter
1 tbsp sour cream

1 Preheat the oven to 350°F. Grease and line an 8in square, shallow cake pan with waxed paper. Melt the butter in a pan and stir in the cocoa.

2 Beat together the eggs, sugar and vanilla extract in a bowl, then stir in the cooled cocoa mixture with the nuts. Sift over the flour and fold into the mixture with a metal spoon.

3 Pour the mixture into the prepared pan and bake for 30–35 minutes, until risen. Remove from the oven (the mixture will still be quite soft and wet, but it cooks further on cooling) and leave to cool in the pan.

4 To make the frosting, melt the chocolate and butter together in a pan and remove from the heat. Beat in the sour cream until smooth and glossy. Leave to cool slightly and then spread over the top of the brownies. When set, cut into twelve pieces.

ITALIAN OLIVE BREAD

A traditional Italian bread called *focaccia* made with olive oil and flavored with a Mediterranean mixture of olives, sun-dried tomatoes and dried thyme.

──INGREDIENTS──

Makes 1 loaf
3 cups all-purpose flour
½ tsp salt
1 tsp dry yeast
1 tsp dried thyme
3 tbsp olive oil
4 black or green olives, pitted and chopped
3 sun-dried tomatoes in oil, drained and chopped
crushed rock salt

1 Place the flour and salt in a bowl and sprinkle over the yeast and thyme. Make a well in the center and then pour in ⅞ cup warm water and 2 tbsp of the olive oil.

2 Mix to a dough and knead on a floured surface for 10 minutes, until elastic (or use a food processor or a mixer with a dough attachment).

3 Place the dough in a large oiled plastic bag. Seal and leave in a warm place for about 2 hours, or until the dough has doubled in size.

4 Turn out the dough on a floured surface and knead lightly. Flatten with your hands. Sprinkle over the olives and tomatoes and knead in until well distributed. Shape the dough into a long oval and place on a greased baking sheet. Cover and leave to rise in a warm place for 45 minutes. Preheat the oven to 375°F.

5 When risen, press your finger several times into the dough, drizzle over the remaining olive oil and sprinkle with the salt. Bake for 35–40 minutes, until the loaf is golden and sounds hollow when tapped on the bottom.

ZUCCHINI AND PARMESAN BREAD

Vegetable breads made with baking powder are popular in Australia, America and in Great Britain, too. They are a delicious way to use up a glut of home-grown produce.

────── INGREDIENTS ──────

Makes 1 loaf
1¼ cups flour
1 cup whole wheat flour
2 tsp baking powder
1 tsp salt
1 tsp ground cumin
1 tsp fennel seeds
8oz (2 medium) zucchini, grated
⅔ cup vegetable oil
2 eggs, beaten
3 tbsp milk
⅔ cup grated Parmesan cheese
1 tsp sesame seeds
salt and black pepper

1 Preheat the oven to 350°F. Grease a 2lb loaf pan and line the base. Sift the flours, baking powder, salt and cumin into a bowl and tip in any bran left in the sieve.

2 Add the fennel seeds, followed by the grated zucchini.

3 Whisk together the oil, eggs, milk and half the cheese in a bowl. Stir into the zucchini mixture.

4 Spoon the mixture into the prepared pan and level the top. Sprinkle the top with the remaining Parmesan cheese. Bake for 40–45 minutes, until risen and when a skewer pierced through the center comes out clean. Serve hot or cold.

Welsh Cakes

Pice ar y Maen – cakes on the stone or Welsh cakes – are fruity, spiced teacakes traditionally cooked on a bakestone. They are served warm as a popular teatime treat all over Wales.

─── **Ingredients** ───

Makes 12
2 cups flour
½ tsp baking powder
1 tsp ground cinnamon
4 tbsp butter
4 tbsp lard
6 tbsp sugar, plus 1 tbsp extra
for sprinkling
½ cup raisins or currants
1 egg, beaten
1 tbsp milk

1 Sift the flour, baking powder and cinnamon into a bowl. Add the butter and lard and rub in with your fingertips until the mixture resembles fine bread crumbs.

2 Stir in the sugar and the raisins or currants and mix well. Add the egg and milk and mix to form a soft dough. Knead lightly, then roll out the dough on a lightly floured surface to a ¼in thickness. Cut into twelve 2½in rounds with a fluted cutter.

3 Lightly grease a large heavy-based frying pan or griddle and cook the cakes in batches on a low to medium heat for about 4–5 minutes each side, until golden brown and cooked, yet still moist in the center. Sprinkle the cakes with sugar while they are still warm and then serve at once.

Austrian Raspberry Tart

─── **Ingredients** ───

Makes a 9in tart
1¼ cups flour
¼ tsp ground cinnamon
¼ tsp ground allspice
pinch of grated nutmeg
1 cup roasted hazelnuts,
ground
6 tbsp butter, diced
4 tbsp sugar
2 egg yolks
9 tbsp raspberry jam
confectioners' sugar, for dusting
raspberries and fresh mint sprigs,
to decorate
whipped cream to serve

1 Sift the flour and spices into a bowl and stir in the ground hazelnuts. Rub the butter into the flour until the mixture resembles fine bread crumbs (or use a food processor).

2 Stir in the sugar and add the egg yolks. Squeeze together until a dough is formed and knead lightly. Wrap in plastic wrap and chill for about 30 minutes. Meanwhile, preheat the oven to 350°F.

3 Roll out the pastry and use to line an 8in loose-based pie pan. Prick the base. Re-roll the pastry trimmings and cut into ¼in wide strips.

4 Spread the jam over the base, top with a lattice of the pastry strips, pressing the ends on to the edge of the tart with your fingers.

5 Bake for 35–40 minutes until dark golden. Dust the tart with confectioners' sugar while still warm, decorate with raspberries and fresh mint sprigs and serve with whipped cream.

PEANUT BUTTER COOKIES

Peanut butter is probably the favorite American spread. These cookies are so easy to make and delicious to eat!

INGREDIENTS

Makes 15 cookies
½ cup butter, softened
⅝ cup soft light brown sugar
3 tbsp chunky peanut butter
1 egg, lightly beaten
½ tsp vanilla extract
1¾ cups flour
½ tsp baking powder
¼ cup honey roast peanuts, chopped

1 Preheat the oven to 350°F. Grease two baking sheets. Place the butter, sugar and peanut butter in a bowl and beat until light brown and creamy (or use a food processor).

2 Add the egg and vanilla extract and beat in well. Sift the flour and baking powder into the bowl and mix with a wooden spoon until crumbly. Mix together with your hands to form a dough and knead lightly on a floured surface until smooth.

3 Break off 15 pieces of the dough and roll into balls. Place on the baking sheets and flatten slightly.

4 Press a few pieces of the honey roast peanuts into the top of each one and bake in the oven for 10–12 minutes, until just golden.

5 Remove the cookies from the oven, leave for 1 minute to firm slightly and then transfer with a spatula to a wire rack to cool.

ITALIAN PASTRY TWISTS

Deep-fried pastry twists, hearts or knots traditionally flavored with Vin Santo, a sherry-like Italian wine, are served hot, dusted with confectioners' sugar, at Italian carnival time.

INGREDIENTS

Makes about 40
2¼ cups flour
1 egg
pinch of salt
2 tbsp sugar
½ tsp vanilla extract
2 tbsp butter, melted
3–4 tbsp sherry
vegetable oil, for deep-frying
confectioners' sugar, for dusting

1 Sift the flour into a large mixing bowl and make a well in the center. Add the egg, salt, sugar, vanilla extract and melted butter.

2 Mix with your hands until the mixture starts to come together. When the dough becomes stiff, add enough sherry to make the dough soft and pliable. Knead until smooth and then wrap and chill for about 1 hour.

3 Roll out the pastry thinly and cut into forty 7 x ½in strips. Tie each one loosely into a knot.

4 Heat the oil in a pan to 375°F and deep-fry the pastry twists in batches for about 2–3 minutes, until puffed up and golden.

5 Drain the pastry twists on paper towel, sprinkle them generously with confectioners' sugar and serve either hot or cold with coffee.

INDEX